UNCHARTED TERRITORY

A FATHER'S JOURNEY
R. Manasseh Thornton

Uncharted Territory: A Father's Journey

Copyright © 2025, by R. Manasseh Thornton

ISBN: 979-8-9986869-1-7

ISBN: 979-8-9986869-0-0 (eBook)

Published by R. Manasseh Thornton LLC

Printed in the United States of America

All rights reserved. No part of this book may be reproduced or transmitted in any form electronic, or mechanical, including photocopying and recording, or held in any information storage and retrieval system without permission in writing from the author and publisher.

All real-life anecdotes are told with permission from actual parties involved and recorded to the best of the author's recollection. Names in some instances have not been used at the request of the individuals referenced. In some cases, parties mentioned are deceased. Details of some instances have been slightly modified to enhance readability, or to ensure privacy. Any resemblance of any other parties is purely coincidental.

NO AI TRAINING: Without in any way limiting the author's [and publisher's] exclusive rights under copyright, any use of this publication to "train" generative artificial intelligence (AI) technologies to generate text is expressly prohibited. The author reserves all rights to license uses of this work for generative AI training and development of machine learning language models.

DEDICATION

To my wife who supported my thoughts and feelings from the beginning. **Imani**, thank you for being the vessel that brought our boys here. Thank you for being my wife and my best friend.

My sons, **Elijah Manasseh** and **Caleb Manasseh**, you're the best thing I have to offer this world. You're the inspiration for this book. You are easily my greatest accomplishment.

I want to encourage healthy conversations between us as you grow into manhood. I hope our open communication will help other men have difficult conversations with their partners before and after they have children to ensure they create the space their children need to thrive.

I want you to know that NOBODY…and I mean NOBODY on this planet, will love you more than your mother and I. Nobody will love you like we do. Come to us about anything, no matter what it is…no matter how bad you think it is…we will always love you, no matter what. We can work through anything together. Trust us, because we trust in you. We love you. Forever and always.

Thank you for choosing me to be your dad. I love you more than you will ever understand or comprehend. My job is not to be your friend but to be your father. I will guide you, teach you, support you, discipline you, and love you. I'm here for all of that, and I always will be. I hope our talks, my fussing, and expressions of love, comfort and remind you that I love you to the end and back.

You have a road map of life… go explore.

Love,

Dad

FOREWORD

I had the pleasure of meeting Manasseh in the fall of 1994, my sophomore year at Wilberforce University. He was a freshman, and from what I remember, he was reserved, very unassuming, and friendly, but kept to himself. While he was learning the ropes as a freshman, I, was preoccupied with "the process" of joining the premiere fraternity on campus.

The following year, he seized the opportunity, was selected, and through his journey into the fraternity, it was interesting to watch him. It didn't take much to see there was something different in the way he carried himself.

At the young age of 19, he appeared to be confident and spoke his mind when he felt the need, although at times it may have led to a few nights of sitting in a chair pondering his thoughts…). He later became the chapter's president, a well-deserved position, due to his leadership and the respect he earned from interacting with our brothers.

Manasseh is a man of principle and possesses high moral character (depending on how one defines morality…). I've always admired that about him. He's true, dare I say brutally honest, and a loyal brother. This was apparent in 2015, when my parents, within weeks of each other, died. He, along with a few other brothers were by my side, seeing me through that difficult time.

We have become lifelong brothers and friends and often speak about life as husbands, family dynamics, and the joys of fatherhood. With us being fathers of Black boys in America, it's never a dull conversation. We've swapped stories that dads particularly, know so well: school, sports, opposite sex, future goals, video games, and other extracurricular activities. We've had deeper conversations that continue to play out in the news from the political landscape to untimely deaths of young Black men. How do we as fathers guide our young black sons? What advice or life lessons do we share?

When I got the call that he was writing this book, I was both surprised and excited. This book, reminds me of some conversations we've had over the years, however, it is more personal. Manasseh bears his soul and shares unapologetic thoughts as a father and husband. This book will have you in stitches laughing in one section and cheering him on as if he is Eddie Murphy in the movie "Daddy Daycare" in another.

Uncharted Territory is an interesting take on fatherhood. There aren't many spaces for men to go and talk about how to be the best dad ever. Manasseh addresses his not knowing, to feeling unsure about becoming a dad. His transitions from working with Children's Services, to being married, and deciding to be a stay-at-home dad, gives him a unique parenting perspective that is seldom told. His story should provide men and women safety in knowing, there isn't just one way to lead a family. The value a father brings to his family isn't just financial.

Manasseh has done a great job in discussing topics that are relatable for families. What I love about this book, is that it addresses the pressures of being a parent, the love relationship with your spouse, self-care, and rules of the road for his children. This isn't just a book for dads and their experience, it's a window into an experience anyone raising children and living this thing called life will enjoy.

My hope is that his kids will enjoy their father's journey by reading this book. They have a loving father, who along with his wife, love them dearly, and it shows.

Eric Ford

PREFACE: CREATING A LIFE

There is no such thing as the "American Dream." We all should know by now that they sold us a bill of goods with that one! Inasmuch, there is no such thing as a perfect life. There is just life. Depending on what path you take, it will just be a different life. I don't necessarily believe in a better life or worse life scenario (if I would have taken another direction my life would have been better).

What you make out of your life is your unwritten story and is completely up to you. Sure, you'll have obstacles, barriers and mistakes, but making the best out of the hand you're dealt is what life is all about. You can't help the circumstances in which you were born. You can't pick your parents, your family, or the status you're born into. But you can maximize your circumstance to benefit you and those around you. You do not have to be defined by your circumstances. You can use those circumstances to become a better person.

Growing up I was a hopeless romantic, I could always see myself getting married. Someone who would love me, challenge me, and help me grow. But when it came to the children portion of the equation, I wasn't so sure. Not only was I not sure but having children was a constant internal debate for me. I considered it, but it was never something I had a desire to do. Of course, I'd play with the idea of what they would look like, how they would act, or how they would behave, but I never had a desire to have children. When the notion of having children would come to my mind, it was always filled with this ambivalence. I would ask myself, "Why bring a child into this world of uncertainty? What's the purpose? Is it for me?"

I could never come up with a viable reason to create a life, and the thought of it honestly scared me to death. While working in Baltimore, Maryland for a short while, I met a young man, who was maybe in his mid-20s, who told me he scheduled a vasectomy. I was fairly astonished at how candid he was about not wanting to have children. He said, "I never wanted kids. I don't want to slip up and have one when I feel so strongly about not having them."

In my mind, that was a profound decision to make at such a young age. I shared this story with numerous people, and they all agreed that he was too young to make such a definitive decision.
"What if he changes his mind? What if he meets someone, he wants to have children with? It just doesn't make sense". Well, he felt like his decision would help steer those who wanted children away and attract a partner who

was like-minded. I really envied him for having the bravery and conviction to stand by his decision. I often wonder how it turned out for him. Did he never have kids? Maybe he had the procedure reversed. Or maybe decided to adopt. Whatever his path, his life is likely not worse or better, but I'm sure it's just different.

In my journey, I've come to the conclusion that not everyone should have children. THAT'S RIGHT! I SAID IT OUT LOUD! (YOU SEE THE ALL CAPS! I'M YELLING). If you do not have an overwhelming desire to have kids, my advice is to consider not creating a life. Here's the thing about creating a life. First off, it's the closest thing to being God. It is a surreal endeavor. Creating a life when there was none, in your likeness and image. That's profound to me. Secondly, it's the one thing you can't take back. Marriage is supposed to be forever, but we all know that isn't a reality for everyone. You can make an attempt at marriage, try it out, and then decide it's not really for you.

You can change careers (which is scary), but doable, to leave your comfy and secure job and try your hand at something new. If it doesn't work, you can go back to what's comfortable. Same with moving to a new city, state, or country. Try it and if it doesn't work, you can always go back to what's normal. Creating a life is the one thing you cannot take back. You can't try it out and then decide it's not for you (well at least not without devastating and life-altering consequences for the child).

One of my favorite artists, Yasiin Bey, (Mos Def) wrote these lyrics in his song "Ms. Fat Booty, Part II". I think it represents this point:

"…I guess God was like, aight, fine!

Careful what you wish for,

'cause you just might get it in heaps.

Try to give it back, He be like,

"Nah, that's yours to keep"!

I believe many people don't truly consider the ramifications of creating a life. Yes ramifications! I'm not all doom and gloom when it comes to kids, but real conversations need to start happening about parenting. Some parents are suffering. Some feel like they're drowning, so a discussion is essential. I believe people think having a child is fun. You get a lot of attention. You get a party and gifts! Who doesn't want that? OH, but parenting can also be extremely taxing. Financially, emotionally, psychologically, and physically. It is by far the most difficult job on the planet in my opinion; I call it beautifully challenging. Nothing can prepare you for it and there is no secret to success. It is all an experiment, and the outcomes are varied.

I've seen two children raised in the same home with the same birth parents turn out totally different in life. One became a judge and the other a career criminal. There is no guarantee and no true measure of success. It is absolutely an experiment. I'll try these things and hope my child turns out to be a good, honest, and successful citizen in society. How they get there and if they get there…total mystery. Many would argue that having children is just the next step in the process of life. I believe that thought process is, and has been detrimental to many parents, marriages, and children alike.

Deciding to create a life just because it appears to be the next step in the progression of life shouldn't be the only determining factor here.

Sure, children bring new life, excitement, happiness, and joy. They really are the apple of your eye! On the other hand, they force you to sacrifice time, money, goals, relationships, and freedom. It's not easy. AT ALL (I'm yelling again). In my humble opinion, having children should never be taken lightly. You should think about it, talk about it out loud, and then talk about it some more. There is a FOMO! That's real. I'm not denying that it exists. If you don't have kids and you're talking to your friends, they all have stories about the kids. Practices, recitals, birthday parties, and AAU (UUUGH! Don't get me started on AAU). I can imagine that people can feel like they're missing out on something amazing. People sharing videos of their kid's accomplishments and all that jazz! I'm here to tell you, FUCK THAT SHIT! It's all smoke and mirrors!

Many of those same parents, if they could do it all over again, would NOT have those kids! But if you don't know, you don't know. Listen, if you never really wanted to have kids or you are truly uncertain? Wait. Tell your partner the truth, that you are uncertain, and you want to wait. Take the proper precautions and please just wait. Finding out that you're not cut out for parenting after the child arrives, sucks.

The Purpose Of This Book

I am writing this book because I want to talk to fathers (and parents alike) about the Uncharted Territory of fatherhood and parenting. I have a lot of friends who are fathers. Many of them either didn't have a father in their home, or their father was not always emotionally available or supportive. Our parents didn't have dialogue with us to the degree that we, as parents, are currently having with our children. We are finding ourselves in conversations and situations with our children that we never had with our parents. My generation has had the privilege of spending more time with our children, with deeper conversations, and as a result, we know them more intimately than our parents ever really knew us. So, our relationship with our children is completely different from what we experienced with our parents, and because of that, we don't necessarily have an example on how to navigate *Uncharted Territory* with our kids or partners. The things our parents did and the way they parented (or engaged in relationships) wasn't always appropriate or ideal. Coming to grips with that is paramount, and is a step in the right direction to understand your parenting style.

Let me let you in on a little secret…Fathers many times don't feel supported, loved, appreciated, or cared for. We're raised in this country to be tough and firm, emotionless and stoic. And when it comes to our families, we are to sacrifice for the greater good of the family, no matter what. But that leaves us very vulnerable. Unable sometimes to show weakness or admit when we're lost or don't know the answers.

I have a unique perspective about fatherhood. If you are a parent who feels inadequate and may internally regret your decision to have kids, you're not alone. Some of us were not fearless enough to say out loud, "I don't want to do this!" I am writing this book to give a voice to people who were not bold or courageous enough to express similar feelings and thoughts. Admitting that does not make you a bad person or parent, it opens space for you to address the feelings and begin working through them. For those that never had children, it's okay if you couldn't or had no desire to procreate. You're still whole if you never had children! There is nothing wrong with you. You are not damaged goods and let me let you in on another secret…you're not missing out on much, in my opinion.

But since having my sons, they ARE my responsibility and I have always wanted to provide them with a sort of road map. An account of my feelings, emotions, and mindset along my journey. Along with some advice and support from my point of view regarding life's lessons. I want them to learn more about me and my experiences through my own eyes and with my words.

I hope that this book will serve as a conversation starter for other parents to have with their partners and children. On this life's journey, I've found that opening yourself up to be vulnerable about your feelings and intentions, can clear pathways that make it easier to cope. I hope this book will inspire those of you who read it.

UNCHARTED TERRITORY

CONTENTS

FOREWORD vii

PART I – Unchartered Territory 1

    Here They Come 3

    A Brief Backstory 9

    The Journey 19

    Through The Years 41

    Playdates 47

    From 1 To 2 53

    The Love Of My Life 57

    Why am I Doing This Again? 63

    Help Me! 75

    Love, Discipline, Consistency, And Patience 83

    Insomnia Anyone? 91

Hearing Your Parents' Voice 97

Connecting With Your Children 99

Who Are You Creating A Life With? 103

Partnership In Parenting 109

Recalibrating With Your Partner 115

Who Said Men Are Not Nurturers? 119

Unexpected Turbulence 125

Transitioning 131

Conclusion- I'm A Good Dad 135

PART II - EPILOGUE 139

Things I Want My Sons To Know 141

PART I – Unchartered Territory

"I wanted to ensure that my wife knew I supported our decision, but I'll admit, I didn't know how to feel or process the great news."

~R. Manasseh Thornton

UNCHARTED TERRITORY

HERE THEY COME

My wife and I were married for six years before "we" got pregnant. Initially, we were not trying to have kids on purpose. My wife was finishing up medical school when we met. Her next step was at least four years of residency. So the plan was always to hold off on having children until a much later date. But the moment my wife and I let our guards down and took less precautions we got pregnant.

From the moment we found out, there was a surreal feeling in the atmosphere. One of those out-of-body experience type things. Was I happy? Ehhh, Ummmm. Damn, I really couldn't answer that question at the time. I wanted to ensure that my wife knew I supported our decision, but I'll admit, I didn't know how to feel or process the great news.

The time between finding out "we" were pregnant, and the due date felt like purgatory. There was this reality I saw on the ultrasound in real time that let me know a life was being born, but for me and maybe some other men I presume, there was a real detachment from that reality.

I saw the baby bump, noticed changes in my wife's behavior, eating habits, sleeping patterns, etc. I knew a life was growing in there, but it wasn't a feeling I was able to truly attach myself to. Don't get me wrong, I was fully engaged and an active participant in the process. I was present, helpful, and supportive (ask my wife 😊). She was feeling things in real-time, a totally different set of complications, revelations, and realities, but I had to vicariously experience it through her because I wasn't able to physically feel it. I'm sure that's how nature intended. But there is no switch that goes off to make it make sense.

From the prenatal appointments, to rubbing her belly with oils to keep the skin smooth and elastic. To baby classes where we learned breathing techniques and all, I was totally immersed in the process, but it was a weird experience preparing for a purposefully created life that I never really wanted.

As the baby was growing, we were reading to it and putting headphones on her belly: heavy on the hip-hop, classical and R&B. It still didn't feel quite real to me; a truly surreal experience. As time progressed, I'd see the hand or foot poking through her belly, doing front flips and backflips and such. Literally an alien being was forming in real time. But I never truly felt connected to what was happening. It was a paralyzing feeling.

I found myself constantly thinking about how different our lives would be the moment this life was birthed. Trying to get a grasp of what it meant and what it would look like. Also, all of the things I needed to do to prepare for before the baby came. Painting the room, putting beds, bassinets, and pack-n-plays together. Making sure we had car seats, diapers and formula. At the time it all felt overwhelming.

We had an elective c-section, so we knew the exact date of birth. As the countdown to the date arrived, it felt like I was a spectator in a game that I was supposed to be playing in but for some reason I was watching from the sidelines. I found myself trying to wrap my mind around the fact that before the birth, there was no child and on August 15, 2011, I would be responsible for a life that wasn't there the day before. I pondered, "I don't know how to take care of a child! I don't even want to take care of a child." I thought, "Why in the hell did we do this? What will this even look like?"

I was in a strange place, on a strange road that I had never traveled. To a place I had never been before. I was nervous, anxious, and a little scared. I realized that I was traveling in Uncharted Territory. I don't know if everyone should be a parent. I'm not certain everyone should procreate and raise children. Some people don't have the temperament, patience, or love for the role. In the end, it damages a life that never asked to be here and never requested to be created. In that selfish act, I believe at times, a parent can do more harm than good by creating that kind of life. How can I be a good father when I never wanted to be a dad? We'll soon find out.

"The foundation that my parents laid was solid as a rock. Not only could you stand on it, but you could also build on it."

~R. Manasseh Thornton

UNCHARTED TERRITORY

A BRIEF BACKSTORY

I was born and raised in Youngstown, Ohio, a small working-class town with a deep history in steel mills, car manufacturing, and mob ties. Yeah, deep mob ties. Comedian Richard Pryor once said, "The craziest job I've ever had was working at a mafia nightclub in Youngstown, Ohio."

I grew up the fourth out of five children in a two-parent household. My parents have been married for over 60 years. My dad is 93 and my mom is 86. They are old and OLD SCHOOL.

My dad did not play games when it came to respect and expectations, but he only whooped us if we did something really unacceptable: a call from a teacher, not listening to mom, or breaking something in the house could all be reasons to see dad and his extremely thick leather belt. There was no tolerance for back talk, sass or disrespect. What my dad said was gospel and there was no rebuttal, no cross examination, nor a retort. Those were the rules, and you abided by them or dealt with the consequences. In layman's terms, you got your ass beat and put on punishment. It sounds crazy to say, but back in those days, it was more a reality than not.

Dad was the provider, and a great provider! He worked at the steel mill for 30 years and almost always had several different types of jobs. He was absolutely a renaissance man. A throwback of sorts. He was good at a multitude of things. He could cook, landscape, sew, sing, do hair, was a school bus driver, a fashionista, and did a little construction. We were a house of 7 and we never went without basic needs. You didn't always get what you wanted, but you always had what you needed. Dad certainly showed me how to provide for my family, work hella hard, be consistent and sound in my decisions.

He had some saying that were the concrete that poured into my foundation:

- Don't ever spend all your money in one place.
- You never want to be somewhere you're not wanted.
- Do it right the first time; you won't have to do it again.
- Measure your wants versus your needs.

Mommy was a stay-at-home mom for a while, and she handled day-to-day rule enforcement in the home. She didn't hesitate to dole out punishment when needed. But she, unlike my dad, was more open and understanding at times. If I felt something was unfair, she'd at least have a conversation with me. Even if I didn't get what I wanted, there was room for a discussion. She tried to be fair.

When Mommy was called into the ministry she wasn't at home as much. But don't let the smooth taste fool you, my mother did not play, either! One Sunday during service, when was at the podium in the pulpit, my friends and I were in the balcony chatting a bit too much. I heard her voice bellow over the loudspeaker, "Manasseh Thornton! bring yourself down here to the first pew and sit down!"

"You're going to call me out in front of the entire church?" I thought. I was so embarrassed. Being embarrassed was the least of your problems if you tried Bob or Gena. You did not play around with my parents, unless you had a death wish.

But even with the discipline, there was a real consistency to our household that we were lucky to be raised in. Everyone went to church on Sundays, of course school during the week and a mixture between church events (choir, bible study, youth group etc.) and extracurricular activities (football, baseball, choir etc.). During the week, we ate dinner when my dad got home from work, which most days was between 4-6. Then we'd watch the local news at 6pm, national news at 6:30, Wheel of Fortune, Jeopardy, and whatever was on between 8-9. The kids were in bed by 9:30 p.m. My parents watched the nightly news at 11, and everyone was in bed no later than 11:30. Quiet house. Every night. Consistently.

Weekends we could stay up until 11pm or later, but then it was bedtime. That consistency paired with the love, discipline, and life lessons was a foundation that could be stood on. Not perfect, but it was solid, and in my opinion, it was paramount to my development as an individual, partner, and father.

Were things perfect? Hell no! Nothing ever is. I wish my relationship with my father growing up would have been better. It really didn't feel like a relationship, more of a circumstance. He was my dad, he went to work, worked hard, and provided. But we didn't have the same kind of connection I have with my boys. He never talked to me about girls or threw a football with me. We never really bonded over anything. But being a dad myself now, I realize that connecting with your child can be a difficult and unique challenge. Trying to find something that you both enjoy can take a lot of time and effort. I have one son that enjoys comic books, the other loves basketball. I try to meet them both where they are and try to find a common ground. But it can be difficult to find that common ground as a parent, especially when you may not be interested in what they're interested in.

Communication is key! I think a lot of what I experienced with my dad was the age difference and just being at a different time. But I think some of it was cultural too. My dad was born in 1931, I was born in 1975. There was a big gap and that showed itself in our relationship. Back then, children spoke when spoken to, we stayed out of "grown folks business" and we didn't get involved in the dealings of the household. We were children and that was our place.

If we were struggling financially, we never knew it. One reason is because back then, parents didn't divulge "grown folk business" with children, the way we do today. These days we share so much more with our kids, for various reasons. Many parents of today would rather be transparent with their kids than to keep them in the dark the way many of our parents did us. Some prefer a more friendly approach to parenting, where they believe their children should have a say in the many matters of the home. Whatever the reasoning, we certainly parent differently than our parents. The time was different, the culture was different and so were our parents. Today's parents have much more facetime and interactions with their kids than our parents had with us. For that reason alone, we tend to know our kids a little more deeply. The pure amount of man hours we spend with our kids is 10x more than I ever spent with my parents growing up. The topics of conversations I've had with my 2 boys are lightyears ahead of any dialogue I've had with my dad to date. I'm sure a lot of it had to do with their age, culture and "the times" they were raised.

I was always thankful that my parents decided to stay together, because I knew a lot of my friends didn't have their dad in the home. I was lucky enough to see and experience what married life and raising kids was all about. Even with a dominant father in the house I had a lot to learn about fatherhood.

My dad's parenting style left a bit to be desired. He was tough, no nonsense, and at times unyielding. Never abusive, just to be clear. But there wasn't a relationship beyond father and child. At least not until I became an adult. I recognized that on my journey, so I attempted to cascade nurturing, patience, love, and understanding over my family as a father and husband, but it was a character that I morphed into somewhat on the fly.

I had never experienced a father or man doing what I was trying to do as a stay-at-home dad. My dad was the opposite of a stay-at-home dad, so I knew I had a lot to learn and a helluva hill to climb. The foundation that my parents laid was solid as a rock. Not only could you stand on it, but you could also build on it.

"Why would I bring a child into a world like this?"

~R. Manasseh Thornton

UNCHARTED TERRITORY

THE JOURNEY

After graduating high school, I was off to Wilberforce University (The WU), the first private black institution of higher learning in the country. It was there that I would begin my journey in finding out who Manasseh really was.

Coming from a small town like Youngstown was an interesting experience. A small city, that used to thrive, but by the time I was leaving high school, it was nothing more than an "uncultivated weed of society." A lot of violence, blight and dread. All I wanted to do is get the fuck outta dodge! But I truly didn't know what I wanted to do, or who I really was.

What I did know about myself at that time was this: I was the fourth child out of five. I loved music, I loved to sing, I enjoyed speaking in front of people, and I was certainly more of a lover than a fighter. All I ever wanted to do was fall in love…I know…I know! What a simp! What a sucka! But that's who I was. A true romantic who wanted to experience love and life.

I'm also a Scorpio. Which means I love hard AF, if you do me wrong, I'll never forget and I'm passionate as all hell. What a large lump of clay I was. Young, dumb and full of possibility, lol.

At The WU I gravitated toward a specific Greek lettered Organization that caught my eye on "the yard." Little did I know how influential they would be in my development as a man. Alpha Phi Alpha Fraternity Inc. Mighty Xi Chapter was a rite of passage for the young, militant, naïve, and curious mind that was Manasseh. Alpha took what my parents and family created in me, broke it and refined it into who I am today.

I have two brothers that I love, Kamau and Josh, but this relationship within the brotherhood was different.

Through this kinship, I learned my weaknesses, my strengths, and my potential. Nothing is impossible and I can go much further than I think.

Once I left Wilberforce with a degree in Sociology and minor in criminal justice, my first job was with an alcohol and drug prevention agency back in my hometown of good 'ol Youngstown (uuugh)! I never wanted to go back home, but that's what happens when you don't have a solid plan in place. This would be the first stop along my journey of working with at-risk youth. We offered in-school and after-school programming to get kids to think before they act and to help them make plans for the future.

After leaving there, I moved near Dayton, Ohio and began working with Children's Services as a foster care case manager and adoption assessor. It was there where I would truly get a crash course on all things children and family related. The good, bad, and ugly were all present, front and center. I knew friends who didn't have their parents together growing up, but working in children's services is like getting a sneak peek behind the curtain so to speak. You see and hear things that most people only hear in local or national news stories. But for caseworkers, this is everyday life.

The horror stories of the things people will do to their children and the conditions in which they will expect them to live in was crippling to see. Investigating abuse and neglect is one of the hardest things I've ever had to do. And you may THINK you know what abuse and neglect is, but whatever you think it is, it ain't that! There are levels to this shit.

I remember when I first started the job and began building this case to get a child removed from his birth mother's home. The house was deplorable! Trash everywhere, roaches, and mice. So much clutter that you couldn't get from one room to another. I just knew I was building a case that would be undeniable to ignore.

I mounted my evidence, wrote up my reports and went before the judge. I stood confidently, prepared and fortified. "Judge, these are the reasons this child should be removed. The house is disgusting, etc." I went on and on about how bad the conditions of the home were, and why their child needed to be removed.

The judge stopped me and said, "Mr. Thornton, I hear you discussing the conditions of the home, which appear to be unsatisfactory, but is the child being physically abused?"

"No sir."

"Is the child being sexually abused?"

"Not to my knowledge."

"So correct me if I'm wrong. The child isn't physically or sexually abused and they aren't abandoned?"

"No sir, not to my knowledge."

"So maybe they just need help learning how to maintain a home, Mr. Thornton. We don't uproot children from their homes because you think their home is too dirty for your liking. Help them with some resources and services that may aid them in keeping a better maintained home. That's easier than removing a child from their parents."

Big gulp, tail between legs, walk off very fast with head down. It was just a wakeup call to me that this job would be more than personal expectations and beliefs.

It was also during this time when I really started paying attention to the effects of fatherless homes. Sure, there was dysfunction in homes with two parents, but it was obvious that the homes where fathers were absent were the most vulnerable. When fathers are absent, it throws off the equilibrium of the family. Hell, when any parent is missing, it throws the balance of things off. But this idea that men aren't needed and are expendable is a fallacy. We all need ying AND yang. When you are missing one, something is missing.

The stories just tear you apart and break pieces of your soul away. When you hear of cases where a parent or both parents sexually abuse a child, the child is taken away, only to want to reunite with those same parents. They're kids and don't know any better! All they want is to be with their family. The family that is supposed to protect them and care for them. Instead, they are the ones that prey on their own children.

It is very difficult work. I tip my hat to all the case managers and case workers out there. You do important work, you're not appreciated, nor are you paid enough.

After I tried my had at foster care work, I moved over to adoption. I figured, maybe I would get some more feel good stories and less doom and gloom. Although a little easier, it came with its own set of complications. At the time, there were over 5,000 children in the Ohio system. It's rare that people want to adopt older children. Most people want an infant or a child under the age of five, which is understandable. You figure maybe they didn't have to endure as much trauma when they're younger.

Or maybe they weren't as influenced by their surroundings and circumstances so you as a parent can implement your beliefs and morals in them. Sounds good in theory, but not always the case.

I've seen families get the child they believe they were meant to have and bring that same child back to the agency after a year or two and say, "we can't do this anymore"! This child is uncontrollable. We've tried tons of therapists and resources, but nothing seems to work."

It's heart breaking when you are looking at a child that nobody seems to want. And you know that their road is almost impossible without adequate family and support. There were times when I looked at those children and thought to myself, "Why would I create a life when there are so many children without a home?"

I applaud all good foster/adoptive families and homes (there are not a lot of these for the record). There are also horror stories of horrible foster homes. I used to teach an anger management class and show snippets of the movie "Antwan Fisher." There are definitely horror stories. Unfortunately, anytime money is involved, there will always be some who take advantage of the system.

After a little over five years working in Ohio at children's services, we moved to Detroit and I began working with a new program called Michigan Prisoner Re-Entry Initiative (MPRI).

The concept of the program was to help cut down the prison recidivism rate. I was the program facilitator for our county. We would meet with clients who were set to parole within the next 30 days. We would meet them inside the prison facility, interview them, and determine what resources they may need to prevent them from reoffending. As I began to work with this program, I was hit again with this moment of clarity.

As I was interviewing these men, I felt an overwhelming feeling of sadness. These were an example of the fathers who left children behind on my children's services caseload. This is where all the fathers ended up. Whether it was because of what they'd done to their child, themselves, or someone else.

Prison is full of fathers that if given a chance, a plan, and some resources, could possibly go back and reclaim their families, neighborhoods and communities. A Bureau of Justice Statistics study found that 66% of offenders will reoffend within the first three years and 82% within 10 years. And if you are child of an incarcerated parent, you are six times more likely to end up in the system. I had been in Social Work for about 15 years at this point, and the interweaving dynamics of the system was hitting me particularly hard during this time.

Seeing that the nuclear family was being destroyed daily by drugs, alcohol, violence, lack of opportunity, and discriminatory practices was weighing heavily on me. I never wanted kids, and being around Social Work sort of fueled that feeling even more.

Soooo, fun fact. I taught parenting classes long before I ever had children. Yeah, I know! You're confused. How can someone with no children teach a parenting class? Well, while I was working with the MPRI program, I also started working with another agency called CARE out of Macomb county. They specialized in prevention work. It was there where I taught adult and youth court ordered anger management and eventually parenting classes.

I applied for the job as a second gig to work in the evenings. I was selected for the anger management classes by an amazing social worker by the name of Paddy Laske. She was passionate, aware, and driven to do the work we were called to do, which is to help people in any way we can. Paddy saw something in me and gave me an opportunity to dive into this arena. I would be a contractor with the agency and provide the services they needed rendered.

I started out doing the Anger Management piece, 6-8 week sessions for two hours once a week. And the classes went very well. Paddy would sit in on the classes to evaluate and her feedback was always very comforting. we would frequently brainstorm and she was always open to my off the cuff ideas, which I truly admired and appreciated. She gave constructive criticism, but I always left the meetings feeling empowered.

One day after one of my classes, she approached me and told me that the agency was getting a new contract to do parenting classes, six weeks, two hours a week. Some parents were court ordered and some were just self-motivated to find new information. I looked at Paddy and said, "You know I don't have any children right? Why would anyone listen to me about parenting?"

She said, "You have a way with people and your perspective is a bit different. I really believe the parents will resonate with you." So she showed me the curriculum and asked me what I thought.

I told her, "I don't doubt I can do it, I just am not sure what the response will be." We agreed that I should try it out. She would shadow me and evaluate to ensure things went smoothly. We both taught the first class and it was great. Paddy showed me some tricks and I was able to play off of her set-ups.

After the first round of classes, she took the training wheels off. She sat in the back of the class like she was a parent, no one knew she was the boss. I started the classes by having the parents write their first name on a nametag and how many kids they had. I also had a nametag. Once everyone looked up from writing, they would look around and see who was who. Then they would look at me and be in total astonishment! "You don't have any kids?" someone would always belt out from the crowd. After which, the murmurs and scoffs would ensue. It would make me laugh every time it would happen. It was hilarious to me.

I understood what they were saying, but once I got through half of the first class, I could see their body language changing before my eyes. After the first class, one parent came up to me and said, "I felt like you were sitting in my house, listening to my family, and then came to this class and told my story." That felt good to hear, it's always amazing to learn that you are reaching your clients.

I successfully taught those classes for years, but there was that one thing that I was missing…the experience of actually having a child. But unfortunately hearing these families stories began to further push me away from wanting to have children.

My last stop, before totally hanging up my Social Work hat, was in Baltimore, Maryland. There I worked with an organization that operated group homes. I was hired as group home manager, in charge of 5-7 homes with anywhere from 8-12 kids in each home. This was by far the hardest job I had ever had in my freakin' life! For starters, I'm not from Baltimore, and my only understanding of this underbelly of Washington, DC, (sorry B-more, maybe things have changed?) came from watching The Wire. Yeah, right! I know! And trust me, The Wire was definitely a character study of this place. Because it was exactly that...the Wire.

We had just moved to Baltimore from Detroit because my wife was doing a one-year fellowship at Johns Hopkins. So, I left the MPRI program and we made the decision to move to B-More for the year. The job lasted exactly 30 days.

Working with at-risk youth is such a challenge because you know that it is not their fault they are in the position they're in. The reason they act out the way they do is directly connected to the abuse and trauma they've experienced. You want to help them break that negative cycle, but at the same time, you are fighting against nature versus nurture.

I remember getting hired on a Monday and I think they threw me to the wolves on Tuesday. Starting at 6 am, I would go from house to house to review how the evenings went and speak to the staff on duty before shift change. There was almost never a boring moment. From kids not reporting back to the house, to kids trying to burn the house down, and everything in between.

My first day, I walked into one of the houses and was greeted by a very charismatic youth that we'll call James. James walked into the kitchen and said, "And who might you be?"

"First off, good morning! I'm Mr. Thornton, the new group home manager. And who do I have the pleasure of meeting?"

"Okaaaaay Mr. Thornton! I see you! Trying to be all professional and thangs! Got your 'lil khaki pants on and all." Inside, I was cracking the hell up. But I kept my composure and just chuckled. "James, this is just how I dress and yes, I am professional."

"Well Mr. Thornton, I hate to be the one to let you know, buuuut you'll be out of them 'lil khaki pants before you know it."

With my eyebrow raised I say," James, I ain't new to this, I'm true to this."

James snaps his head back and throws his hand over his chest in shock and awe, "OK MR. THORNTON"! I proceed to explain to him my resume and how I've been doing this kind of work my whole life.

James snickered and countered, "Mr. Thornton, NOBODY survives this! Yo ass will be gone just like all the rest of 'em! TRUST!"

I said, "You seem so sure of yourself, but ain't no fear over here." We both smirked and kept it moving. BOY! Little did I know, James ass was a prophet! That job kicked my ass! I stopped dressing up for work (just like the prophet said) and started coming in with jogging pants, tennis shoes and war paint on my face. I looked like Rocky Balboa training for a fight with Ivan Drago, "if he dies, he dies."

I was dressing for war, because that's exactly what it felt like. For 29 straight days, I was in hell. I was on-call 24/7 and rarely had a quiet night. One night, around 2am, I get awaken out of my sleep with a call from a house monitor.

"Hello?" (whispering)... "Mr. Thornton, this is Kate, I need you over here right now."

"What's going on?"

"The kids are going crazy in the house, so I locked myself in the bathroom."

"WHAT!?!? Get out of the bathroom and assess what's happening."

"I'm not leaving this bathroom until you or the cops get here."

So I get out of my comfy bed and drive over to the house and walked in. The scene was like something out of the movie "Animal House." I stood in the doorway for what had to be 10 minutes, just staring at the destruction. I was so furious I could barely speak. What came out of my mouth next was a tirade of epic proportion. One of which I cannot share with you due to the fact that it was 1, unprofessional, 2, profanity laced and 3, totally inappropriate. But at the time it was absolutely warranted. I was only at the job for 30 days because when they hired me, they needed me to start right away, but I hadn't had time to get a physical done. Policy stated that you had 30 days from the time of hire to get a physical done or you would be taken off the schedule until completed. I didn't realize that until they reminded me on my 29th day.

"Mr. Thornton, don't forget to get your physical, or we're going to have to take you off the schedule until you do." That job had broken my spirit so badly, that on day 30, I went to get my physical and never went back.

My wife said, "You just have to quit this job! It's killing you! I've never seen you like this." That's because I'd never felt like that before. Social work is a challenge, but I've never had to quit a job because of how hard or difficult it was. I certainly had never quit a job without having another one already lined up. But this was different. That gaddamn Prophet James tried to warn me, but me and my 'lil khaki pants didn't listen. After that stint, I was done with social work for a while.

THROUGH THE YEARS

When Elijah, our first born came, it was a rush of euphoria. What a life changing event. I'm not sure what I looked like from the outside, but from my point of view, I was KILLIN IT! Feedings, diaper changes, floor time and playtime…I was on it.

The blob stage of this process sucks so bad. You don't realize how much it sucks because you're new to it; trying to find your way. Once you settle in a bit, you realize they are dependent on you for every fucking thing! YOU CAN'T EVEN HOLD YOUR DAMN HEAD UP!! Come on man, work with me here.

I'd prop him up on some pillows and make a fort so he wouldn't fall the hell over. But every time I start to walk away…sliiiiiide, plop. I was scared to leave the room half the time. If I needed to get something from another room it felt like I was playing a game of Double Dutch.

Waiting for my turn to jump the hell out of this loop and jump back in before it was too late.

This is the stage of the TRIFECTA! Pack-n-plays, car seats, and strollers. Oh, dear gawd! If I ever have to assemble another pack-n-play I may just drown myself. Early on, that was the job. Trying to create a loving and nurturing environment so that they can thrive, grow and prosper. This can be a wonderful stage of the process. As babies, they smell soooo good! I used to bury my face in my son's neck and just breathe in the essence of his scent. That new baby smell! It was like a new car scent! They can be so adorable. But as the kid grows, that new car scent fades and then, it starts smelling stale and stanky!

Being that my wife is a physician, she worked a lot. I did a lot of the heavy lifting early on. When she'd be on call on weekends, I'd pack the baby up and drive from Michigan to Youngstown on a whim. It got me out of the house and once I got home, I could get him situated and then let my parents or siblings give me some reprieve. The 3 ½ hour trip would be amazing for the first 2 ½ hours. I'd play old school hip-hop and R&B (with no cussing). A little alternative and jazz. Elijah would be so happy until we got about an hour away from my parents' house. Then he'd start crying and crying and crying.

I'd stop to feed and change him, but he wouldn't stop crying. He'd cry until he'd throw up. Then I'd stop again to clean him up. The 3 ½ hour trip sometimes took five hours. When he got a little older and was able to talk, we found out that Elijah gets motion sickness. It was then that we realized he was getting nauseous in the car, especially when watching the iPad. Little things like that are incredible parts of parenting. Things you can't prepare for or dictate. But as they grow, you grow, and as they learn, you learn. You teaching them about the world and them teaching you about yourself.

"Introducing certain energy to your children can have a negative or positive effect on them. So don't be too eager about inviting everyone into you and your child's world."

~R. Manasseh Thornton

UNCHARTED TERRITORY

PLAYDATES

As Elijah got older, of course playdates begin to rear its ugly little head. Once you put your child in any kind of preschool or program, you're going to get this… "Hi, my name is (fill in the blank), are you Elijah's dad? Sebastion has been talking about this kid Elijah every day after school and he keeps asking me if he can have a playdate."

UUUUGGGHHH! Listen, I understand and appreciate the world of playdates, I really do! But as a parent, these things suck worse than drinking a thick milkshake with a narrow straw.

First of all, I'm a 6'1, 230 pound black man (who isn't half bad looking). One of the best parts of it all is that I would always have to remind the requesting parent that I'm a stay-at-home dad.

For example, I went to pick Elijah up after preschool one day and all of the parents are standing around. A father comes up to me and says, "Hi, my son would like to have a playdate with Elijah. If it's ok, I'll take your number, and my wife can contact your wife and discuss the details. They can meet at our house or at the park, whatever is most comfortable for her."

I had to politely inform this gentleman, that my wife is physician, and her schedule is very fluid. "I'm a stay-at-home dad and I will be the one scheduling the playdates. So, if it's ok with you, give me your wife's number and I'll call her and set it up. We can meet at the park or like you said, at your house. It should be fun." I really use to get a kick out of that.

Playdates to me, are a gift and a curse. On one hand, you want your child to begin developing relationships and friendships. It's also great to have something planned, something on the calendar to do, to break up the monotony. But, trying to create new friends as an adult is hard work! Our kids may get along, but what if we as parents don't vibe? It makes for an extremely uncomfortable situation. Elijah would say, "Dad, can I have a playdate with Kirk? He's my best friend" (because everyone they meet is their best friend at that age).

Normally, I would gladly set-up the playdate, it gives me a little break from being the only source of entertainment. But I don't really like Kirk's parents. I'm sure it's me and not them (which is what we always tell people we don't want to be around…it's me, not you). But I didn't like their energy or aura.

So what do you do? Your child really likes this kid, and you want to make them happy and create those bonds. Well, I started backing away from those playdates. My schedule suddenly tightened up and there just didn't seem to be enough time in the day to get together anymore. Little did they know, I was cheating on them with another family. A family I grew to be extremely fond of, and I didn't regret it one bit.

Listen, trying to find friends for your kids can be complicated. But don't be too thirsty out there. Accepting any and everyone's invitations because some people's energy or vibe may not mesh with yours. Introducing certain energy to your children can have a negative or positive effect on them. So don't be too eager about inviting everyone into you and your child's world.

I also would like to say a word to certain parents, some people are raised differently than you and not everyone has the same trust and or value system that you have. I am speaking specifically to parents whose boundaries appear to be a bit skewed.

One time, I had a parent from my son's first grade class, that I did not know text me the following message: "Hi, I'm Devon's mom. He's been talking about your son Caleb since the beginning of school. Devon wants to have a playdate with Caleb this Friday, so I can pick them up from school and take them to our house. Let me know if that's ok."

UUUHHHHH HELL THE FUCK NO THAT'S NOT ALRIGHT!?!?! I have never met this woman in my life! I don't even know what her name is, because she introduced herself to me through text message as Devon's mom. WTF is going on out here? I come from a culture where you have to meet people, see where they live, how they live, and who they are before a child is spending time with them. I'm not letting my child go to a stranger's house, under any circumstances.

As a stay-at-home dad, I looked forward to the breaks that some playdates afford. But I would never put my child in harm's way for a couple hours of reprieve. So, parents, before you offer to take another person's child (that you don't know) into your home, properly introduce yourself to them. Invite the child and the parent to your house. Break bread with one another. You may notice that you guys don't really get along and future playdates aren't necessary. Or, things are safe, expectations have been discussed, and boundaries have been set.

My son never made it to Devon's house. And they never had a playdate. FOH.

FROM 1 TO 2

After we had Elijah, he's a little over a year now and my wife is starting to discuss having another. I never wanted to have children so, I was thankful that he was a healthy and happy child. No need to poke the bear. But we both came from big families and we both recognize the importance of having a sibling if possible. If for no other reason than it takes the pressure off of you as a parent to be their only source of entertainment. Just sayin'.

So we did decide to give it another try. We got pregnant almost immediately after being intentional. But unfortunately, we lost that child. Miscarriage, another conversation that's hard to have and a bit taboo. But in my opinion, it's a necessary conversation to have.

For women, I can't begin to understand how complicated, difficult and painful that experience has to be. I won't even try to articulate that experience from your perspective. But from my perspective, again, it's difficult to comprehend. I was sad, but I was mostly sad because my wife was sad. I didn't experience any part of that growing process and so it was hard for me to be in the same emotional and psychological space she was in when it happened.

I really had to monitor my emotions and adapt them to whatever space she was in. In my mind, we have a healthy child right here that needs our attention, affection and care. Let's just celebrate this. But the reality of course is, it's easier said than done. She wanted to try again, immediately and by our surprise "we" got pregnant almost instantly. So, we go from one, to two and everything changed…again. With multiple children, things become a little more chaotic. You repeat all the dreadful parts of early parenting…again! Insomnia, head fog, car seats, and cribs! UUUGGGHH! But the second child does give the first child someone to play with and that my friend is priceless! I loved watching my oldest attending to his baby brother, trying to share his toys, and making him laugh. It's really cute until they get a little older and the laughing turns to arguments, fights, and selfishness. We always knew that if we had one child, we would at least attempt to give them a sibling/playmate to go through life with. We were lucky and blessed to have 2 healthy boys who are smart, charismatic, talented, and beautiful. I hope that they remain close and connected. They are their brother's keeper, and we try to instill in them the importance of family and having each other's back.

"I've loved my wife since the day we met."

~R. Manasseh Thornton

UNCHARTED TERRITORY

THE LOVE OF MY LIFE

I've loved my wife since the day we met. We met at an Irish pub called the Dublin Pub in Dayton, Ohio. Neither of us wanted to be at that particular venue, but we were both kidnapped by our respective friends at the time. We met that night and have been together ever since.

When I approach a relationship, I try to give myself fully to the experience. Relationships are not 50/50, they should be 100/100. I have to give my all to my relationship to make it work and hopefully my partner is doing the same. Open communication, honesty, and realistic expectations should be the foundation of any viable relationship. It takes time to develop, and there are certainly some growing pains involved, but the journey is well worth it. Because marriage is hard as hell and in my opinion, if you're going to have any chance at all you have to incorporate a solid foundation. A true friendship.

Once I met my wife, we constantly had the conversation about if we were going to have children. Early on, we weren't interested in having kids. Our normal conversation when discussing having kids would be, "Naw, we're good right now." That statement rang true for the first six years of our marriage. As time progressed, my wife started hearing her biological clock getting louder. Pregnancies and childbirth get more complicated the older women get. I understood that, but I grew accustomed to our lifestyle as a childless couple. Freedom, travel, less distractions and more one on one time with each other, was the life without children. But should we have a child just because time is of the essence?

Hard Conversations

The conversations were not easy, but they were plentiful. We started having "family meetings" during our dinner dates. We would discuss family goals, expectations, whether we were satisfied and happy. We'd discuss everything from bills, to vacations to sex. Nothing was off limits as far as our family discussions. It was a semi-safe space to discuss everything regarding the family. I say semi because feelings would get affected by what was said sometimes. Some of those dinners…and rides home were as quiet as a mouse pissing on cotton. And when it came to the topic of children, we were both non-committal.

Neither of us could get the other to make a strong decision either way. Total ambivalence! No one wanted to truly acknowledge that they did not want to have kids. I certainly never desired to have them and internally that had never changed. But eventually it turned into, "if we're going to do it, we better try to do it now."

I cannot overstate how important and vital these conversations are. It at least establishes some expectations, goals, and desires. Even if they're not always met, at least you have a map of accountability you both can go back to and trace your steps. One difficult conversation that happened for us was when my wife asked me if I would consider staying home and taking care of our first son. It was honestly something I had never considered. I was flattered that my wife had the belief in me to even ask me. But what would that look like? I didn't even want to have a child and now I'm going to be a stay-at-home dad?

There were so many thoughts running through my mind, but one thing was for certain, he was my child and I have no problem taking care of mine. I obviously considered what my friends would say and the jokes that would ensue (although, they were all very supportive). But the main thing that I wanted to discuss with my wife is how she would view this arrangement? How would she handle her physician colleagues and her friends, who would definitely have some questions and jokes. Would SHE look at me differently being a "homemaker" and all? She quibbled early on that I was far from a homemaker! (eye roll)

But my wife assured me that she didn't have a problem with it and was secure and fortified in her position. For her, it would serve as peace of mind for her to be at work and not worry about the baby. Knowing he was with his father and being taken care of was one less stressor for her.

I told her, "As long as you can look your coworkers, friends, and family in the eye and not be the butt of a joke, then I'm onboard." It was a hard conversation, but a necessary one.

It would scare the shit out of me to go into life changing situations with people and not discuss the possibility of things. Sometimes we're so afraid of rocking the boat that we just stay quiet. But we all know what happens when we sweep things under the rug. That monster rears its ugly head at the most inopportune time. We start to build up resentment and regret and those things stick to your psyche like superglue.

Suppressing it won't make it go away; you'll just have to fight the fight again at a later date. Open up and have meaningful conversations about the things that are important to you both. And if you can't come into alignment about anything, then maybe you have to reconsider your approach or even your partner.

WHY AM I DOING THIS AGAIN?

I know many people who have always wanted to have children. They knew at what age they wanted to have them, how many they wanted to have, and sometimes the more the merrier. It's as if they innately were always supposed to have children; like it was some type of divine intervention. Some of those same individuals have an uncanny way of making parenting look EASY.

For these people, parenthood is beautiful, amazing, painful, stressful, fun, scary, intense, and wonderful. I say they make it look easy because we ALL know that this shit is a long way from easy. I've never heard a person every say that parenting is easy.

Why do we procreate? To keep the family legacy and name alive? Natural human order? To have someone love us unconditionally? Are we creating children out of pure selfishness? Do we want someone to take care of us when we're old? Do we need a child to help fix our broken relationships and marriages? Well, I can't answer life's multitude of questions, but I hope we can explore these questions along the way.

If you have children, do you remember what life was like before they came along? It was most certainly different though. One of my pet peeves is when a parent exclaims, "I couldn't imagine my life without my kids. I don't remember life before they came". FOH! As the young folks say, "that's so cap bro". I damn sure remember what my life was like! I remember being bathed in the pure essence of sweet freedom. Waking up on the weekend when I felt like it, instead of being up at 7 a.m. for a little league game.

The overbearing sound of silence echoing throughout the house. AWWW! Sweet unadulterated freedom! Those were the days. How about hemorrhaging money like I've been shivved with an icepick by an inmate on the yard. My wife and I started thinking about how much money we would have saved (or spent) if we didn't have kids and I threw up in my mouth a little bit.

Listen, I will give my disclaimer for the people who may be outraged by my wording. I love my children more than life itself. I would sacrifice my life for them without hesitation. But you guys have to help me. I just don't see the point of having these little rascals. I mean, what do I get out of this deal again? A little mini me who highjacks my freedom, finances, relationships, and life! Only for them to tell me I don't know what the hell I'm talking about half the time? All in the hopes that one day they MIGHT make something of themselves and not be an eternal dependent? Oh, let me guess, I'm hoping that They MIGHT take care of me when I'm old and needy? Maybe they won't put me in a nursing home?

I know, I know! I'm a horrible parent. But I'm just thinking out loud, sharing some personal thoughts that have creeped into my jaded mind. I just had to be honest for a minute before I head back to reality.

Lose Yourself

There's a MAJOR shift that happens when that child arrives. And some hard realities are exposed. I discovered in this process of having children that I'm a selfish SOB! I thought I knew I could be a little selfish, but having kids smacked me right in my selfish ass mouth.

It's hard as hell to be selfish when you're a parent or a partner though. And what I learned along the way was that the only way that I could exist in the confines of marriage and family dynamics was to assassinate my ego daily. I'm talking about looking at yourself in the mirror, taking your ego and blowing it to smithereens. Your ego can't survive in this environment, if you want to be a responsible parent and partner. I am attempting to be a responsible parent. Whether right or wrong, I prioritize my children's needs before my own. I lose myself in them and for them and sometimes that is exhausting and overwhelming. I've absolutely lost myself in this process of fatherhood.

Since they were born, I feel like I haven't been able to think of anything except them. It has chipped away at the essence of my being because my identity has changed under the role of "Dad."

There is an underlying anxiety that coincides with the intense heart palpitations I experience being a parent. I have never worried so much in my life. I even get lost in the worrying! Their safety, what they're learning, what they're not learning. What they are consuming, whether it be food or social media. I question if I'm pushing too hard, or not hard enough? I wonder if I'm crippling them or giving them wings? I think about their gifts and their limitations. It's all encompassing and at times debilitating.

These are just some of the questions that swirl around my head and I know you have your own. These thoughts began the moment they arrived and that feeling (I can imagine) never goes away. It's the reason I am writing this book. I know that I am not the only person feeling these unpopular feelings and emotions. This angst that sits in the pit of your stomach and never truly goes away. That feeling is the same feeling I had before we had our children. I could feel the responsibility, pressure, and angst before considering children and always asked myself "why in the hell would I do that to myself"? But here I am, trying to figure it all out.

I lost myself in the space between not having children and having them. I turned myself into something that I had never seen in my life. There is a quote by John

Green, "the nature of impending fatherhood is that you are doing something that you're unqualified to do, and then you become qualified while doing it." That quote rings so true to me. The repetition of the days run together like a stampede and it certainly can begin to feel like an endless game of Groundhog Day. The walls start to feel like they're closing in on you. There were times when I would feel like I couldn't breathe and just needed to leave the house for some air and a change of scenery. Walking around aimlessly in a dept store or grocery store just to get some time away and breathe. Not even sure what you're doing or why you're doing it. On top of that, you can begin to lose your confidence.

For some reason, you can begin to feel undesirable and lonely. I was with a child all day, when my wife came home from work, we'd maybe have a couple hours together to eat and discuss the day and then she was in bed because she had to go to work the next day. As a physician, sometimes she would just want to decompress once she got home. Her days are stressful and she deals with life and death constantly. Sometimes she doesn't even want to talk. So where does that leave me? There were a lot of days when I wouldn't have any fruitful adult conversations, no one to talk to, just me and the baby.

Literally dealing with an infant day in and day out is utterly exhausting. OOOHHH MY GAWD! They need and want EVERYTHING! It's so fucking frustrating! They'll throw up on your favorite outfit, eat your favorite meal, and work on your favorite last nerve! But in that comes lessons that can curate you into being a better person. Learning patience (beyond understanding), unconditional love and selflessness will help anyone become a better overall human being. But it is hard work!

I once had a conversation with a couple who loved playing tennis together but stopped playing when they had children. They talked about their love for tennis and how they both played in college. I could see the passion come back to the gentleman's face as he talked about his time on the court. But since having kids, they exchanged the tennis they loved so much, to play pickleball (throw up emoji) because they could incorporate the kids in it as well. When speaking with the dad further, I could tell that he really missed playing tennis. "Why can't you play anymore?" I asked.

He responded, "I just can't find time."

Well, my wife and I play tennis together several times a week. We make it a priority to play tennis together whenever we can. It's OUR thing. We've taken our kids to go to the park with us and they play amongst themselves while we play tennis. It doesn't make you a bad parent to put your needs above your children's wants sometimes. Sometimes our kids, society, and even our own self-talk tells us that we are wrong for placing some of our personal desires over our children's. But I say fuck that! We are individuals too! We are here to have a life experience as well and it all can't just be child related shit.

Now finding that balance is again a tough road to travel. But you have to remind yourself that your desires and needs matter too. Maybe at the time they're not as immediate as the needs of your child, but you don't have to give up your life, to lovingly care for others. Carve out some time for individual activities as well as activities with your partner. It serves as a refresher so that you can focus once you're back in parent mode.

It's vital for stay-at-home parents to have a hobby or an outlet; something to change the pace of the day. Also, a good support system helps. You need to lean on those that you trust and that love you. Ask for help when you need it and trust me, you're going to need it.

"Asking for help is complicated."

~R. Manasseh Thornton

UNCHARTED TERRITORY

HELP ME!

Asking for help is complicated. You don't want to appear weak. You don't want to be a bother or burden to others. But we all need help. Ironically, the need for help doesn't always showcase itself right away. You can feel like you're handling things, but when the feeling of really needing help hits home (sometimes in crisis mode), it can be extremely overwhelming. Help comes in many different forms and takes on a variety of shapes.

Having someone watch your child for two hours, once a week can release some levels of anxiety. It gives you something to look forward to and also allows for a break in the routine. You should never do chores or run errands on your 1-2 hours of down time. That time should absolutely be geared towards self-care, reflection, wind down and recharge. If you're doing chores or work during a rare break, it will feel like you've never left your post as a parent.

The other mistake some parents fall into is even on date nights or times when help comes, we are constantly worried about the child/children that we never relax, relate, or release. Especially when dealing with the first child. All parents believe their first child is made of fine China and could break or be harmed at any turn. It's typical for first time parents to be overly protective of their first child.

But as other kids come, some of that "white glove syndrome" goes out the window. You're less patient, less afraid, and less extreme (at least in most instances). But trying to secure help, before the shit hits the fan is the key. You should have a plan of action for when you feel overwhelmed, sleep deprived, anxious, and or angry. Maybe it's a neighbor, or a relative or a work friend. You never want to lean on people too much and become a burden, but asking for moments here and there to help your mental, physical, and emotional health is essential.

An Unwelcome Guest (Postpartum)

A topic that is not always discussed enough in my opinion is postpartum depression. This is something that I did not recognize at first, but it presented itself in our marriage. I started noticing that my wife seemed a bit sad and depressed. Everybody has some bad days, but this was lingering. Being tired all the time is baseline for my wife, but this was definitely a different space for her.

Nothing seemed to make her happy for long. She constantly thought she looked fat and undesirable which led to constant wardrobe changes before we could go out anywhere. Sometimes, she would try four to five things on, come out of the bedroom in her robe and say, "I'm not going."

She used to always be up for a night out or a good time, but again, this felt different. I was under the impression that when a woman had a child, that a portal of motherly instinct, understanding, and patience just opened and poured motherhood all over them (ha!). What I learned is that giving birth affects everyone differently. Some women have "easy" pregnancies. No sickness, no pain, etc. Some have high risk pregnancies, where they must see their doctors regularly, and stay on bedrest.

But what is clear is that the process of carrying a child and giving birth affects a woman in a variety of ways. I'm not a woman, but speaking with my wife and some friends and family about their experience has given me insight on how difficult things can be for women.

She has a little alien being growing inside of her belly for nine months, literally sucking up all of her nutrients, resources, and all the shit she needs to survive.

Then it grows in size and weight, putting pressure on all of her organs, weighing her down.

Although the experience is beautiful for many, the process can be physically, emotionally, psychologically, and spiritually challenging for the others. So, there are a lot of variables at play.

It can be a complicated experience and because of that, there can be "side effects." Because a woman's body is being inhabited, it doesn't always adjust to its previous form. Personal body shaming and insecurities can play a huge part in a woman's attitude and behavior.

Wearing black all the time because every other color makes them look "fat." They don't always feel pretty or attractive which can affect their self-esteem. They may not want to be intimate because they don't feel beautiful.

As a husband, I wasn't prepared for some of the effects of pregnancy. People don't talk about these types of obstacles when discussing marriage or parenting. I think it is important to have these discussions because it helps arm you with information that may get you through some of these difficult circumstances. As a partner, how will you handle it if your partner is bedridden during the pregnancy?

Are you prepared to do the heavy lifting around the house: cooking, cleaning, and helping her? What if your partner doesn't want to be intimate during pregnancy? What if your partner falls into a depression after giving birth? How will you handle discussing the issue and dealing with it? It can be very frustrating for everyone involved if the mother of your child experiences postpartum. But again, open communication and patience are the buzzwords for the day.

Postpartum has many different faces and different effects on women. Having open and honest conversations about how each person feels is very important. Men, do your best to alleviate stress from your partner's everyday life by being present, helpful, and aware. This will help you help her throughout this process and hopefully will alleviate some stress for you too.

"Love, Discipline, Consistency, And Patience,

These are what I like to call

the four pillars of parenting."

~R. Manasseh Thorton

UNCHARTED TERRITORY

LOVE, DISCIPLINE, CONSISTENCY, AND PATIENCE

These are what I like to call the four pillars of parenting. If you're missing one of these things, your life may not be balanced. But good luck on being able to do all four effectively. Parenting is complicated and layered.

What is Love?

Every parent SHOULD love their child, right? But that love varies depending on different circumstances. For instance, how the child was conceived, or who the partner is plays a role in how you love your child. Did you and your partner break up, or stay together? Does your learned experience and behavior impact how you love your child? You must also ask yourself:

- How was I loved when I was a child?
- Did I feel loved? Safe? Considered?
- Was my voice heard?

All of those questions play an integral part in how you parent and how you show your kids love and how you accept love from them and your partner. Love and patience are the only worthy adversaries against evil and negativity.

What is Discipline?

Discipline is another variable in the equation. This to me is one of the more complicated variables in parenting. How do you disseminate discipline? Telling your child no seems easy but it is difficult to do consistently. You can't say yes to them all the time.

They need to understand what no means and how to handle that. Because as responsible parents we know that life will tell everyone no from time to time and it would be in our best interest to know how to handle it when it bares its face. Plus, if you left it up to the kids, they'd eat candy for dinner, stay up late, and be on their phones or games all day. Oh, they're already doing that? Lol, this is why the discipline variable is so important. We have to prepare them for life; discipline is vital for success. Why would we deprive them of that amazing trait?

So many times my kids put me in a position to say no. "Dad, can my friend come over? Can I go over to their house? Can I have a sleepover? Can we go to the trampoline park?" Listen, I don't want to ever do the shit that kids do, but I do understand I have to do some things the kids want to do, it's my job. But I don't have to do everything they want to do.

I'm the parent and I have to set parameters and expectations. So, saying yes to everything, or not setting reasonable expectations can come back to bite you. And to bite you, I mean like sitting at the trampoline park with five kids wishing you were anywhere else but there.

Discipline Can Go Too Far

When my oldest son was about five, I spanked him because I believed that he had peed on himself purposefully. During the spanking, he looked like he was in despair. He couldn't understand why I was spanking him. I remember being angry, but I wasn't sure why. I had dealt with bedwetting, and I believe those memories and experiences crept up in an ugly way. Midway through the spanking, I stopped spanking him and began weeping uncontrollably. I didn't want to discipline my son in that way. It felt wrong.

Because I had been spanked, I thought that was the way I was supposed to parent my kids. People say, "Spare the rod, spoil the child," but that thinking is short-sighted and damaging. There should be a consequence for bad behavior, but for me, physical violence isn't the answer. I know a lot of parents that struggle with how to discipline their kids. Especially the ones who came from "disciplinary" type homes.

How do you correct your child without physical consequences? I would suggest that you get creative. Think outside the box. The punishment doesn't always have to be doom and gloom. Depending on the severity of the infraction, you can have a little fun with it. Don't take yourself too seriously for every little thing. There will be plenty of lessons where you will have to be serious in your approach. When you can lighten it up a bit, you should. This is a skill you'll certainly have to learn with patience and time.

What is Consistency?

One of the most difficult pillars is consistency. As I said before, parenting can be exhausting. Moreover, attempting to keep your parenting style consistent can be a struggle. Children have a way of wearing you down to the point of exhaustion. But it is in those moments that you have to keep the ship steady and stay the course. For example, if you have a rule about poor grades and the punishment is that your child can't use their electronics for the next week. Well, that means you are responsible for making sure they stay off the electronics and keep them busy with other tasks, chores or homework.

After a while, even the parent can get tired of keeping up with the punishment, but being consistent helps not just you, but your child. There is an expectation in place and they know you will follow through, whether good or bad. Being consistent with bed times, meal times, and homework keep you and your child on a schedule. It helps build a foundation and a routine that can help everyone involved. It takes time and patience to be consistent but overall will benefit the process.

Patience

Now this pillar here is a tough one. This pillar buckles regularly for me. Having patience is a true skill that must be developed if you weren't born with it as a gift. Building patience is like trying to build muscle—it takes time and a lot of hard work. Children will absolutely try your patience. I've found myself screaming at my kids like a crazed maniac sometimes! Making threats and demands all while foaming at the mouth like some kind of rabid dog. What I have gathered is that you can't combat children with anger, it just doesn't work. If your parenting style is led by fear or anger, your pillar of patience is buckling, trust me. You need to find ways to be open and accepting and have less closure and denial.

"The only way you can put your best foot forward as a parent and partner is to make sure you are okay mentally, physically, and emotionally."

~R. Manasseh Thornton

UNCHARTED TERRITORY

INSOMNIA ANYONE?

Insomnia and the effects of it are one of the most incredibly heinous parts of parenting. There is nothing that can prepare you to be up with these little needy humans, day in and day out. Feedings every couple of hours, changing diapers, bouncing them, walking them… you name it, you have to do it to entertain them and to get them to sleep.

Every child is different and for some kids, getting them to fall asleep is not always as simple as it seems. A child is tired, gets fed and changed, so it should be ready to fall asleep. NOT SO! At one point, my son didn't like being laid in the crib in his room. He would cry for what seemed like an eternity. Standing up in the crib, holding on to the rails and just wailing like I just set him off to sea alone. Allowing your child to cry sometimes, is an extremely difficult process to explore. Some parents feel like their child should never feel angst, unpleasant or uncomfortable feelings.

I believe that children should be challenged and taught certain lessons. One of which is laying down without being attached to me. One regret I hear a lot of parents talk about is not making their child sleep in their own room. Children will get away with whatever we allow them to get away with. If we constantly give in to their every wish and demand, I believe we do more harm than good. Children need to know that there are boundaries and expectations. As well as getting them comfortable with being told no at times. It took about a week of me letting my son cry himself to sleep, then he started getting comfortable with laying down and taking naps in his crib.

When your child finally falls asleep, try to get some sleep at the same time. At first, I would try to catch up on chores, while the baby slept. But for me, catching up on sleep was paramount. For one, while doing the chores, sometimes you can wake the baby up. 😩 That's a no-no! Also, doing chores while the baby is asleep doesn't give you any reprieve. You don't give yourself a break. And in my opinion, you have to give yourself little breaks and small outlets.

Caring for a human that relies on you for every single thing, all the time, can be overwhelming. It doesn't always present itself as being overwhelming initially. Over time, frustration does build up if you don't have outlets.

I remember a time, when my oldest was a few months old and unbeknownst to me, I was reaching a breaking point. I was so exhausted! Mentally, physically and emotionally. Since my wife worked and I was staying at home, I made it my job to never bother my wife in the middle of the night. If she has to get up and go to work, I will take care of feedings, changings and night entertainment. Once she was done breastfeeding, she never had to get up at night and take care of the baby. Ever. But with that, comes some exhaustion and I was absolutely tired. Now that we've experienced Covid-19, "Covid Brain" is the only thing that I can closely relate it to. I was in a fog and didn't know what day it was, or how long I'd slept, if at all.

Did I shower today? Brush my teeth? How long have I been wearing this outfit? It was bad! It was just all bad! At some point, I finally get my son down for a nap (after crying for 20 mins straight) and I was going to get something to eat. While sleepwalking through the kitchen trying to figure out what I could eat fast so I could just lay down and get some rest while my son was asleep. I decided on a bowl of cereal.

I grabbed the bowl, poured the cereal and retrieved the milk from the fridge and poured it. As I took a couple of bites, with my head in my hand, exhausted, I noticed that the cereal had an odd taste. So now, I'm annoyed and tired, because the milk must be sour. "GREAT! Another fucking thing gone sideways," I thought. But upon further investigation, the milk wasn't spoiled. Actually, I hadn't put milk in the bowl at all. Instead, I poured my son's formula in the cereal!!!.

"WTF!?!? How could I have done something so stupid?" The formula doesn't look anything like regular milk. I'm sitting there at the table dazed and confused. What's going on??? Then, I got pissed off because I realized that I poured quite a bit of that expensive ass formula in the bowl. At that moment, I realized that I was fried! Like a bologna sandwich fried. I immediately went to lay down. That moment taught me insomnia is undefeated.

Listen to your body and allow yourself time to rest. You need it, deserve it and its essential to you and your child's wellbeing. Nobody is a super parent. We all have flaws. Taking a break, a breather and nap doesn't make you weak. It doesn't mean you can't handle it. "When cares are pressing you down a bit, rest if you must, but don't quit". That line in the poem "Don't Quit" by Edgar Albert Guest speaks to just that.

No one is expecting you to be able to do it all, all the time without fail. The only way you can put your best foot forward as a parent and partner is to make sure you are okay mentally, physically and emotionally.

Get rest, listen to your body, listen to your heart. Talk your frustrations out and take a nap!

HEARING YOUR PARENTS' VOICE

Whether your parents were amazing parental examples or not so much, their repeating voice, their lessons, achievements and downfalls all helped shape their voice. That voice or the missing voice has been speaking to you since your birth. Naturally when you're out on your own and living life, those voices that raised you or were influential in your life will speak to and through you. Whether good or bad, those messages are the "angel" and "devil" on your shoulder giving you advice. Your upbringing and beliefs have to help create your voice through your own experiences. It's your responsibility as a parent to find your own voice.

You must be able to acquire the good things you've learned, discard the bad things you've experienced, and create a unique voice that will leave an imprint on your legacy…your children. We all have a voice worthy of being heard, it's your duty to curate that voice.

How can you raise your child without making some of the mistakes that were made with you? How do you break the chain of neglect or abuse? Where do you learn new skills and techniques to be a responsible parent? You have to recognize that your parents may have done the best they could, but they weren't perfect.

They made mistakes and missteps that may have negatively affected our point of view, or experiences in life. The moment you realize that they are imperfect, the sooner you can begin your journey of imperfection. We're not here to be perfect, we're here to learn and adapt.

Our parents made a ton of mistakes, as will we. But again, it's your responsibility to curate your voice to create new and appropriate responses to your children. And not to fall into the same traps as our parents did.

CONNECTING WITH YOUR CHILDREN

While talking to a friend he mentioned, "I'm afraid of possibly straining my relationship with my son because I can't connect with him on certain levels." This man is my friend and our boys are friends. I could relate to him. I keep hearing this narrative from parents. Many have told me how the disconnection has caused distance between them.

My generation was raised differently. I didn't have a good relationship or connection with my dad until I became a grown man. We didn't do anything together. We didn't have a relationship outside of being father and son. We are choosing to parent our children with a different perspective. When you include technology and social media, this is a challenging time. Our kids are more advanced when it comes to information consumed.

Many of us "old heads" are trying to find ways to have better relationships with our kids in spite of the plethora of distractions. Having open discussions and dialogue. Trying to keep the line of communication open. And, you have to be prepared to answer uncomfortable questions you may not know the answers to.

Creating that bond is not always easy. If you're not a great communicator, or if you were raised in a home where relationship building wasn't a priority, how do you begin to change the narrative when you don't have the skills or skill set? Many fathers want to have healthy and open relationships with their kids, but don't always know how to go about doing it and doing it effectively. One thing that is important is to have conversations with them that are safe.

Conversations where they are allowed to speak openly and honestly without fear of retribution. We expect our kids to have the tools and social abilities it took 30-40 plus years for us to learn and adapt to. To expect my 12-year-old son to understand the depths of my conversations without the experiences that I've been able to incur over time is unrealistic.

Sure, our jobs are to give them road maps and skills that will prevent them from making the same mistakes we may have made, but they still have to get experiences through their own decision making. When your child is talking, use active listening skills to stay engaged. One of my biggest issues is that I hate talking to kids, and the shit they are telling me, I feel like I already know.

Patience is imperative in allowing my sons to open up and express themselves honestly. They are telling me a ton of information, it's up to me to decipher through that info, ask follow-up questions and meet them where they are.

The complexities of our adult experience as dads are lost in their youth and adolescence. Here's the other part, as men, sometimes we think we're going to make our kids into little versions of ourselves (whether good or bad). But our kids are nothing like us because their experience, landscape and timing is different. Frustration can settle in parents when our children aren't behaving how we think they should. We think, "They're not as tough, not as hungry as we were." They won't be because they didn't experience the same things we did. We should be thankful for that.

WHO ARE YOU CREATING A LIFE WITH?

When speaking with couples, whether married or not, something that I hear all too often is a statement that sounds something like, "I didn't realize it would be like this" or "if I only knew." In those discussions, what I'm finding is that people aren't having real dialogue about partnerships and/or parenting prior to getting married or having children.

What appears to be happening is during the "courting" or dating phase, everyone is putting their best foot forward, trying not to initiate red flags. Wanting to be liked over wanting to be accepted. What people don't realize is that the dating experience is when you should be your most honest and authentic self. It helps weed out a lot of riff raff. Give a person a direct look inside your life, good, bad or indifferent.

Even when you get past the initial stages of dating, you should have real, concrete conversations about beliefs, philosophies, cultures, and styles (parenting styles, spousal style, family history etc.). What I'm hearing in a lot of relationships is that some hard conversations were not had early on. When you are meeting new people, you need to stop trying to be perfect and just BE! BE honest, BE yourself, BE vulnerable and BE authentic. "What if he/she doesn't like me if I'm too honest at first"? You're asking me, what should you do if you tell someone who you really are good, bad or indifferent and they don't like the person you present?

I'd say, "Goodbye! Good riddance! Beat it! Kick rocks!" In my opinion, you dodged a bullet, saved some precious time and maybe even some heartache.

We have to be honest with not only ourselves, but with our partners. Without fear of backlash or retribution.

We have to discuss our expectations, fears, desires, wants and needs. That way at the very least you start your relationship off with a foundation of honesty.

Picking a partner to procreate with is a very big deal. I believe some people may take that assignment a little too lightly. The parenting process is hard enough as it is, without adding additional and unnecessary drama by choosing a partner who is not on the same frequency. You have to ask yourself some hard questions:

- Do our thoughts, ideas and beliefs align?
- How are we with money?
- What are our individual goals and the goal of the potential family?
- What's their family dynamic? Do they get along with their family?
- Do we both have the same disciplining style? And if so, how?

It's imperative that when choosing a partner, you should truly consider them wisely. Finding people who are in sync with your beliefs and ideals. Someone who is vibrating on the same frequency or a touch higher than yours. Because not only will you be sharing yourself and your space with them, but you may also be sharing a child. I always tell people to be careful of the energy and frequency they receive and create.

I had a female friend who got pregnant by her boyfriend. I asked if they planned on getting married and she scoffed! "Hell no!" she exclaimed.

I said, "Why are you so adamant about that?"

She said, "He isn't marrying material."

I questioned her, "He's good enough to create a life with but not good enough to share your life with?

She stared into my soul and said, "Shut up, Manasseh!" We laughed, but it's a real question to ponder.

But when you do finally choose a worthy partner, treat them like you chose them. What I mean by that is, don't take your partners for granted. We pick people to share our lives with and sometimes treat them like we don't want them there. What good is it to share your space with someone that you claim to enjoy, but treat them like you don't? So, treat your partners like the gift they are. You chose them, so act like it.

Why would you decide to start a life with someone that you don't even like or get along with? You should be caring for this person, looking after them, picking them up when they are down, holding them up when they are tired and praising them when they are successful. You chose each other, love on each other and take care of each other. Otherwise, what's the purpose?

"It takes a lot of hardcore communication, active listening and understanding to be able to individually move as a unit together."

~R. Manasseh Thornton

UNCHARTED TERRITORY

PARTNERSHIP IN PARENTING

My wife and I try to approach our marriage like a business partnership. Because once the "warm and fuzzies" wear off, you still have to cultivate the relationship if it has any chance at surviving. We have family meetings to plan for the year ahead (trips, events etc.), discuss expectations and if goals are being met.

Although difficult at times, it is important to be open to any topic of discussion. It can be hard to hear someone else's truth especially when it confronts a behavior within us that we may have to change. But asking questions like, "are you satisfied in the relationship"? Or "is there anything I can do to make our experience together more enjoyable or satisfying" shows engagement and the awareness that a relationship is at play.

There is work involved in maintaining a relationship, real hard work! You can't just ask the questions without being willing to do the work to try and address the issues. We are born individuals; we spend most of our life trying to find that unique individuality and where we belong. And somewhere in our journey, we find a soul that we would like to share our space with. But it's complicated sharing and incorporating your personal, private space with someone else. So you go from this personal individual journey to sharing your space, your desires and dreams. It takes a lot of hardcore communication, active listening and understanding to be able to individually move as a unit together.

You have to respect the other person for being an individual, not someone you own, or have rights over. This person had a single path before you met, they'd walked on that path a long time before meeting you. And now your paths have crossed and you are deciding together (hopefully) to move in the same direction. It's not fair to expect a person to not think and/or be an individual first.

So then you add to that, trying to create space in your life for a child, which is a totally different dynamic. Turning off your selfishness is a complicated balancing act in and of itself. You go from being totally selfish to having to consider others before yourself - all the time. It can throw off your equilibrium. So many questions can run through your mind:

- How do I successfully balance my own wishes, needs and desires with the needs of multiple other people?
- Who taught me to do it? Were they successful?
- Is it possible?
- How do I determine the priorities?
- What if I don't want to?

Both parties should be doing their very best to help ease the stressors that accompany having children. If you create a life, a vow has been enacted and expectations abound. It is each person's duty to carry their cross and move the unit forward.

In my opinion, as men it is our duty to do whatever we can to ease the stresses of our family. We should be making things easier and more manageable and not more complicated and confusing. Being considerate of your partner's time, energy, and well-being will go a long way in showing your appreciation. If you are a stay at home parent, are you helping your partner or making more work for them?

Your partner should not have to tend to the children during the evening hours if they need to be sleeping. They shouldn't have to get up in the middle of the night to change diapers or feed the child. When they come home from work, allow them time to unwind and decompress. Each person plays a role in the operation of the family. If you're not an asset you are a liability.

Each individual must pull their weight to make progress for the unit. If one person isn't carrying their weight, it causes cases of imbalance. The person picking up the slack can certainly have unaddressed feelings of regret or frustration. Ask yourself these questions:

- What are my expectations for being in a relationship?
- What do I think my role is in it?
- Am I holding up my end of the bargain or am I reneging on my promises?
- Do I intend to make sacrifices for this relationship?
- As a man, do I expect my partner to take care of all the "household" needs?

If you have an archaic perspective on relationships let me let you in on a little secret…those old ass paradigms aren't working in today's society. Women aren't barefoot and pregnant anymore! They are CEO's, doctors and entrepreneurs. Social media has changed dating and how we meet people. The norms of old are just that…old. We have to adjust our behaviors and expectations accordingly.

Life has changed; our roles have changed. Men, we have to be better. We have to love our partners better, communicate better, and be more attentive.

Women, you have to know what it is that you want and communicate it effectively. We are not perfect and we are not mind readers, but as your partner, we are capable of providing you with what you need if we are aware of your expectations and communicate them.

RECALIBRATING WITH YOUR PARTNER

As we are all aware, relationships are full of ups and downs. It is so easy to take each other for granted and lose some of the frequency that drew us together. We get into the daily routine of life, get distracted and forget to pour into each other the way we need to for continued growth. Reconnecting or recalibrating with your partner can be one of the most satisfying things in the world when you open your heart and mind to it.

When we are going through the motions of life, it can feel like we lose each other. But it's not that we totally lose each other, sometimes we just have fallen out of alignment with each other. It happens to cars, companies, your body, partnerships, and marriages. You can move as a machine for so long that the tires will need rotating or replacing and so will the struts and brakes.

Relationships need room for recalibrating. The frequency we were once on has weakened. It doesn't require a full overhaul, just some minor tweaks and adjustments. Then you can hear and feel the clarity. It is so important to revisit things that connect you and also open yourself up to things that will expand you. Things can seem so much worse prior to communication.

If you allow your thoughts to keep playing an insignificant narrative in your head and spirit, it will. Talking about fears, hangups, and expectations is just a conversation. It doesn't need to be, and shouldn't be, a deal breaker. Within a partnership, individuals should be able to openly express themselves without backlash and judgment. Once those discussions can be had, it opens up portals of understanding that can alter your entire perspective. Have you ever felt like there was no way out of a situation? No possible solution? Just to realize that there is a solution that you didn't consider because it was obstructed by your personal point of view?

Discuss your fears and reservations out loud with your partner. Getting those thoughts out in the open will help you in putting the puzzle together to find the answers you may be looking for, which will help lead you back to each other. Tend to your relationship like you would a plant. When you see your plant with leaves dying off, you have to recognize it needs attention. Take off the dying leaves to initiate room for new growth, new leaves. You may have to repot the plant because its roots have grown too big for the pot it started in. Talk positively to your plant, water it, put it near sunshine. All those things will help ignite new growth and new possibilities. The same as tending to your relationships, cultivate it and it will produce the benefits that you need and desire.

"When men are able to assume an equal role with women as caregivers it becomes most evident that they can nurture as well as women."

-bell hooks

UNCHARTED TERRITORY

WHO SAID MEN ARE NOT NURTURERS?

In this country, most men are raised to be providers, bread winners, the head of the household. But one thing that may be missing at times is the nurturing part of fatherhood. It's as if some of us believe that we can't be nurturing. Sure, we can't give birth or breastfeed, but we can damn sure hug, kiss, hold, be understanding, patient and loving to our children. We have to embrace and be comfortable being vulnerable.

You think you're so manly that you can't perform certain responsibilities or duties? Get over yourself! Toxic masculinity is very real. Unfortunately, it's been over used and weaponized, but it is a real thing. It's a trait men truly have to look within and begin to heal themselves from.

And guess what?!?! If I hear one more man call taking care of his child, "babysitting" I'm going to strangle the life out of him. You are not BABYSITTING your child! You should be taking care of them, because that's your responsibility. To nurture, you have to be vulnerable and egoless.

"Child raising is not an innately feminine thing."

-Bo Pryor

Putting someone else's needs above your own and softening yourself emotionally to help, protect and nurture this little human being is important. Whether that means changing diapers, allowing your partner to get rest while you take care of your child, feeding the baby etc. These traits are necessary for providing a healthy and open environment for your child and family.

This idea that because we're men, we're incapable of providing our children with the softness and love they need and deserve is absurd. I know men that won't hold a newborn baby because they think they'll crush it or hurt it in some way. Stop it! You're not Thanos!

Societal norms will convince you that women have one type of skill and men have another. Some of that is true, but the reality is, men and women are like a Venn diagram, which shows the relationships between concepts. We all come to the table as individuals (a circle), but when we decide to share our space with someone else, our circles overlap. You're no longer just an individual, you are a collective. Some lines blur and some are distinct.

I believe the overlapping circles that we create (the blurred areas) are the areas of vulnerability and

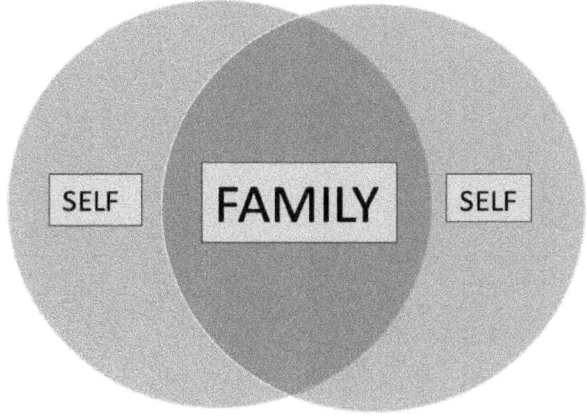

selflessness. As men, there will be times when we must

enact our inner nurturer. Using compassion, communication, and understanding to navigate these unfamiliar waters. It's not only important, but it's also essential. Whether you like the term toxic masculinity or not, it is a real thing. The idea that if you show any sort of vulnerability then you're not a real man, is old, tired, and over. Showing vulnerability makes you human, not soft or insignificant.

Holding your child's hand, giving them a warm hug, and kiss, cheering them on at an event, or consoling them when they're sad, makes you a caring human. None of that makes you soft, it makes you a responsible parent.

"Attempting to explain the emotional trip to hell and back is almost impossible."

~R. Manasseh Thornton

UNCHARTED TERRITORY

UNEXPECTED TURBULENCE

As I was writing this book, my family was hit with an unfortunate and unforeseen circumstance. One day I received a phone call from the principal of my kids' school. My youngest son was in the principals' office. "What in the hell???" I thought. "He is never in trouble in school." My youngest son is a model student for the most part. He is respectful, polite, he participates in class and the whole nine. But there we were, on the phone with the principal for what appeared to be a serious lack of judgement on his part.

He had read a student's story on the computer and decided that it wasn't good. He offered to help them rewrite it, but they declined. It agitated him to the point where he felt he wanted to make a statement, so he deleted the story off of the computer. His punishment was to serve a detention for one day after school the following week. I assured the principal that this was certainly an isolated incident and they would not have a problem out of him again.

What would the home punishment be for such an infraction? Electronics taken away for the weekend (we only let them use their devices on the weekends, to reduce the lack of concentration) and no friends for the weekend. This in my mind was not a major infraction, but misbehavior should have a consequence and we try to be consistent with that. On their way home from school, I received a call from my oldest son in a panic. "Dad, Caleb jumped off the bus at the wrong stop and started running!"

"WHAT?!?!?" Once I realized that he got off the bus at the wrong stop, I immediately ran out of the house and drove towards where he got off the bus. For the next hour and forty-five minutes, I could not find my son. I had obviously called the police who responded quickly. They created a grid which had officers posted at different intersections of the area.

Attempting to explain the emotional trip to hell and back is almost impossible. I literally went through all seven stages of grief within a two-hour period. Losing a child is one of the most sickening feelings I have ever experienced. I've been sad, I've been heartbroken, I've been shocked, and scared for my life. But you can put all of those emotions into one and it still can't describe the space I was in and the pain that I felt when I couldn't find my son. There was a movie that came out in 2013 called Prisoners, with Hugh Jackman. If you've ever seen that movie, I believe it details the emotions fairly accurately.

It sounds crazy to say out loud, but I'm trying to be transparent. The feeling I had when my son was missing, is one of the reasons I never wanted children. I knew that one day I would feel that feeling for whatever reason and in that moment, I kept saying, "this is exactly why I never wanted kids…because of this feeling right here!" It was a personal and internal thought that flowed through me, nobody could hear it, but it was present.

As I'm driving around looking for my son, I have all of the windows down and I'm screaming his name out of the car, CAAAALEEEEB!. The reverberation in my voice as it bellowed for the safe return of my child, was literally shaking my spirit to the core. I was screaming so loudly that the very vibration of my vocal cords, made me begin to weep uncontrollably. My son was missing and I felt completely and utterly helpless. If you've ever lost a child, I assume you may understand what I'm saying. And, if you've never lost a child, I hope you never experience the feeling.

It never leaves you.

The local police department did a phenomenal job of dispatching several units to find our son. And after a grueling two hours, they had found him running down a nearby street. We were obviously relieved, but still shaken. After they found him, my wife took him home and I sat in the car. I couldn't move. I felt paralyzed and for the next 15 minutes I cried like a baby. Trying to figure out how and why we got to that point. And, how in the blink of an eye, your whole world can be flipped on its head.

After we all settled down from the commotion of the day, I had to take my dad hat off, and put on my social worker cap for a moment. Just to ensure that my son was not dealing with something deeper and more alarming. After several days of discussion and reflection, we all came to the realization that this was an isolated incident that was triggered by his fear of getting in trouble and he made a bad choice. According to my son, he panicked and made a decision that will stick with him for a lifetime. He assured us that he has certainly learned his lesson and will become a better person because of the experience.

TRANSITIONING

Legacy is something that I never cared about or considered. Until one Thanksgiving when my father made a declaration that shocked the shit out of all of us. Our family tradition during Thanksgiving is to create a circle around the table before dinner as each person takes a turn sharing what they are thankful for.

Well, when my oldest son was about one or two, we were at our annual family Thanksgiving circle and my dad slowly began to give a disclaimer, "I love each and every one of my children, grandchildren, and great grandchildren. And I'm thankful for all of you. But my grandson Elijah, has a special place in my heart."

As I heard the words flowing from his mouth to the unsettled ears around the table, my eyes grew as large as grapefruits! "WTF is going on here!?!?!" I thought.

"Did he just publicly proclaim my son as his favorite grandchild???"

I shot a deer in the headlights glare at my wife, who was simultaneously shooting one right back at me. I began to sweat as I panned the room at the rest of my family who were giving me the death stare with snobbish disdain.

Although we laugh about it now, I'd never considered that legacy meant so much to my dad. I hadn't realized it until that moment. My siblings all have kids, but my sons would be the only ones left to carry on the Thornton name. And now that he's reached the ripe age of 94, I understand more clearly his sentiments and the weight that it holds.

When we had our first child, one of my biggest wishes was that my parents, who are older, would at least get the opportunity to have a relationship with them that they would remember and cherish. My boys are 14 and 12 now and they absolutely have an amazing connection with their grandparents. I'm so thankful for that as my parents reach the precipice of life. Because as our elders begin transitioning, it is imperative that the rights of passage get passed down to our children. Creating that relationship with my parents ensured that the legacy of our family and community lives on through my boys.

"Our stories may be similar, but your perspective is different than mine."

~R. Manasseh Thornton

UNCHARTED TERRITORY

CONCLUSION- I'M A GOOD DAD

When I began writing notes and thoughts down about how I was feeling, the book's title was initially, *I'm A Good Dad, But I Never Wanted To Be*. That was the raw feeling I felt at the time. After reading this book of my journey, some may be saying, "I feel so bad for his kids! Why would he say such things?"

Well, I've been honest about my internal conversations in hopes that they may help someone else on their journey. I started writing down things during our first pregnancy all the way through the end of this book. It's been 14 years in the making and I will continue to add chapters as I learn and live the excursion.

I love my sons with all of my heart. They are both beautiful, charismatic, funny, smart, and talented young men. I would not trade my children for any of your kids! My thoughts about parenting are not an indictment of me or my children, they are simply honest feelings and thoughts that I've had regarding parenting and life.

It was difficult to come to this crossroads on whether to write a book or not. But I honestly believed that I could not be the only person feeling the way that I felt. And if that was true, then I wanted to tap into that and create a safe space for dialogue. For those who are contemplating whether to be a parent or not, I want you to get real words and advice, not just the normal parent fluff. Sure, you love your children, sure they bring joy. But is it something YOU are supposed to do? Is it something YOU really want and desire? Are YOU prepared for the ups and downs that await? An open and honest conversation, that's all I can ask for.

Thank you for taking this walk with me. It means everything to me that I got this story out and that it may ignite conversations, questions and dialogue. We are all on our own personal journeys and our stories are uniquely our own. Our stories may be similar, but your perspective is different than mine.

Own your truth and take your walk, through this *Uncharted Territory*.

"I wanted my children to know personal things about me, through my lens and my perspective."

~R. Manasseh Thorton

UNCHARTED TERRITORY

PART II - EPILOGUE

I started writing *"Things I Want My Sons to Know"* because I felt like I didn't know my parents that well. My parents are older and the relationships between parents and children was different back in the day. We talked about "Grown Folks Business" earlier in the book, and that was the format many of our parents used. But, I wanted my children to know personal things about me, through my lens and my perspective.

"Things…" is a collection of thoughts, beliefs, feelings and life lessons. You may agree with them or disagree with them, but they're mine and for MY kids! No, I'm joking. I did write them for my boys, but I felt like it may help parents start their own conversations with their children about their feelings and beliefs.

Many of us talk to our children and give them advice and stories. I wanted my boys to have something of a roadmap; something they can hold, something they can read to remind them of me. Whether I'm around or not, they can always return to these bullet points and reset and breathe. I encourage all parents to create something similar for your children. This is my bible to them—The Book of Manasseh, enjoy.

THINGS I WANT MY SONS TO KNOW

- I've loved your mother since the day we met. We met at an Irish pub called the Dublin Pub in Dayton, Ohio. Neither of us wanted to be at that particular venue, but we were both kidnapped by our respective friends at the time. We met that night and have been together ever since.
- At the time you both were conceived, you were created in an environment of love. The atmosphere and the tone of events that created you, were created in love and with love. It's important to me that you know that. The energy surrounding your creation was loving.
- We attempted to raise you with a strong family foundation, with the family first mentality, we teach you to be respectful, kind, tolerant, and multifaceted.

- Men look people in the eye, say what they mean and mean what they say.

- Always do what you think is best, in the moment. Sometimes you don't always have the luxury of time and you need to make a quick decision. Trust your instincts and go with your gut.

- Some people lead, others follow. Whatever your path, be the best at it.

- You are responsible for yourself. Your body, your spirit and your mind. You can't control how others think or act. But you have total control of your responses and actions.

- Try to limit the amount of major screw ups you have in your life. Nobody is perfect, but you can't make major mistakes often and expect to make significant progress.

- Operate at a high frequency and energy level. You'll attract what you put into the universe: positive thoughts, feelings, vibes, and people.

- Try your best to be honest. You'll have fewer entanglements when being honest with others.

- Be kind to yourself and to others. Negative self-talk is toxic and talking negatively about others is equally as toxic. Be kind, it doesn't cost you anything.

- People can take kindness for weakness, so even in your kindness, be mindful that some people will take advantage of that.

- Be true to yourself. There is only one you, don't ever try to be like someone else. So many people wish they had other people's lives. But in reality, you can only live in your truth and authenticity. You are beautiful and as unique as your fingerprints. Follow your heart and live life to the fullest. NO REGRETS.

- Never stress yourself about what you don't have. Always appreciate what you do have while striving to do better.

- Step out of your comfort zone at times, it will help you build character. Change is not overrated, it is understated.

- Don't let your mouth get you into something that your ass can't handle.

- Don't gossip or spread rumors and half-truths. It will come back to bite you in the end. It's irresponsible and dangerous to spread lies and or rumors about others. Remove yourself from those situations if possible.

- It's hard to stand alone when the crowd appears to be moving together. But if you don't believe or know the truth. Don't speak on it.

- Women are the most beautiful and complex creatures on the planet. They will confuse you and amaze you all at the same time. Always treat them with respect. But understand that respect is earned.

- Have a lot of fun. Life can be serious and heavy at times, and too short. So enjoy yourself…A LOT.

- Love hard, work hard and play hard. Life is short and complicated, so enjoy it every chance you get.

- Always be aware of your surroundings. Don't walk around life with your head down or too high in the sky. Always watch what is going on around you.

- Whenever possible, don't sit with your back to the door. You should always be aware of who is coming in and have an eye on an exit.

- Walk with confidence. In life, when you walk around with your shoulders slumped and head down, it gives off the energy that you are insecure and/or incompetent.

- Never be afraid of another man. We are all human. Never give someone power over you by showing that you are afraid of them.
- Never let a man put his hands on you or anyone you love. Violence is never the answer, but sometimes it is a necessity. You have a right and a duty to protect yourself and your family.
- Integrity is essential. Don't ever trade it for anything.
- Laugh…a lot.
- As your dad, I love you more than you will ever understand or comprehend. My job is not to be your friend, but to be your father. Guide you, teach you, support you, discipline you and love you. I'm here for all of that, and I always will be.

- Don't ever be afraid to be alone. Being with someone you care about is amazing, but learning how to be comfortable with yourself is equally as awesome.
- There is an old saying, as a leader "would you rather be loved (adored) or be feared (hated)? Choose your path wisely.
- I am in love with music. I couldn't and wouldn't live without it. Music has always been and will always be here. It never leaves you. Good music is from the heart. It's from the soul. From the source.
- Your mom would likely be successful in whatever she does. She's driven and focused when inspired. She's tactical, organized and competitive. She's a horrible loser but prepares herself for success. Her strength is in her preparation.

- I think that I'm a wanderer by nature. At times, I feel like a drifter. I like to move around and not only do I enjoy change, but I also embrace it.

- I get bored easily. I engage fully into something and at some point, I get bored with it and move on. This isn't a great quality to have, but I've recognized it is a part of who I am.

- I am lazy at times. It's something that I've struggled with most of my life and I try to push myself through it. But sometimes I lack drive. Complacency is a disease that needs to be eradicated from your life.

- One of my biggest regrets in my life is not taking better care of my physical body. I was overweight for a good portion of my life, and I was unconscious about being healthier. After reaching 340 pounds, my largest weight ever, I made a change. Physically, mentally and spiritually. My mom gave me the book, *The Power of*

Now by Eckart Tolle. That concept changed my thought process considerably.

- Many of us take life for granted (being in good health, relationships etc.), but life has a way of jarring you from your comatose state. Death, loss, heartbreak and betrayal are life altering events. Appreciate life and the good things it brings, because the hard stuff is coming, and you'll wish you had peace from the good times.

- Religion: as an individual, it is your responsibility to search, educate and inform yourself about all religions before you commit yourself to something (if you decide to commit). Religion is complicated, make sure that you do your due diligence to find where you belong in it, if you so choose. Although I grew up in religion, I do not have any formal concrete belief. I guess you can call me agnostic. We as humans were obviously created somehow, because all things come from something....a beginning, a source. But the concept of how or by whom is beyond my mental or spiritual capacity. I don't have the answers to why we're here or how we got here. But since you're here, it is your job to live this life given to you with vigor and passion. No regrets.

- In life, you have minimal control in this world. What you do have control of is yourself and your reaction to things. Spend your efforts maximizing the portions of your world you do have control of. Frustration will ultimately show its face when you constantly try to control the things you have no power in controlling.

- To live life to the fullest you should: use the resources, information, experiences and people that you find along your path to help guide you. These tools and individuals will be your compass to guide you to where you envision yourself being in life. As parents, we have provided you with a solid foundation to use as a steppingstone to your own success. Use all of your tools.

- You can't expect everything to go your way all the time. Keep your expectations realistic, not unrealistic. Sometimes you will be inconvenienced…deal with it.

- You never force yourself onto anyone, especially women. If someone says no, stop or they are not interested, please let them be.

- Grandpa gave me sound advice a long time ago that I still live by today. "You never want to be somewhere where you're not wanted". If people treat you poorly and act like they don't want you around, find a space where you feel comfortable, safe and appreciated. You never have to stick around and be someone's punching bag. Stand up for yourself and understand your worth.

- Math, science and language arts are subjects that will fortify you with a solid foundation. You can sprout in any direction once your base is solid.

- "An idle mind is the devil's workshop" is a quote that speaks to what happens when you don't fill your time with positive and productive activities. When you're bored, your mind will find things to entertain it. Sometimes those things are not productive or helpful.

- Being genuine, passionate and true to yourself are skill sets that are vital in building integrity.

- Love and patience are the only worthy adversaries against evil and negativity.

- Try your hand at multiple things in life. The more variety you offer yourself, the more (windows of) opportunities you'll have to choose from. Pay attention to the things that bring you joy and excitement. Your destiny or strength may come from an area close to your passion.

- There is no such thing as the "American Dream". No such thing as the perfect life. There is just life. Depending on what path you take, it will just be a different life. What you make out of your life is your unwritten story.

- Some of my favorite comedians: Paul Mooney, George Carlin, Patrice O'Neal, Chris Rock, Kat Williams, Richard Pryor and Dave Chappelle

- Some musical artists that I admire and love: Stevie Wonder, Bill Withers, Michael Jackson, Luther Vandross, Daryl Coley, Donnie Hathaway, D'Angelo, Erykah Badu and Jill Scott

- Favorite Hip Hop artist: Rakim, Biggie, Tupac, Nas, Roots, Tribe Called Quest, Scarface, Outkast, Little Brother, Jay-z, Kool G rap.

- Be loyal to your family and true friends, they are the relationships that truly matter.

- ALWAYS take care of your mother. You only get one, you owe her your life and you must cherish, respect and protect her.

- Learn to forgive yourself. No one is perfect and you will make a ton of mistakes, but you can't live life in constant regret. Understand you are human and imperfect and forgive yourself for your mistakes. Move on and do your best not to make the same mistake twice.

- In life, you must have a level of tolerance for people who are different from you. No two people are alike and that's what makes us individually phenomenal. Respect the differences in people and allow them to be themselves. Talking to and learning from people who are different from you builds growth and depth.

- There is positive energy and negative energy. The one that you give the most attention to will be the one that will yield the most power. Be careful of your negative thoughts and feelings, they will manifest into reality just like positive ones.
- There is good and evil in the world. Be cautious of those who choose evil, there is nothing they aren't willing to do.
- You shouldn't say things about people behind their back that you wouldn't say to their face.
- Social media is not life. Be careful how you operate in the social media space. Don't post things that are inappropriate or personal. You can't take the information back once you've posted it and people

will use that information against you when it benefits them.

- "Don't judge a book by its cover." Explore things and people in life. You can't think you know someone based on how they look. Get to know people before you cast judgment on them. Not everything is as it appears.

- Watch and listen more than you talk. You'll learn so much.

- Time is the only thing that can heal pain. Give yourself time to get over break-ups, disappointments and loss.

- Real life is complicated and amazing. Social media is not life, (likes and dislikes) it's fabricated, and unreal. Navigating real relationships is real life. Loving, losing and experiencing human contact and interactions is real life.

- Each of you has something unique about you. Call it your imprint or personal fingerprint. It's uniquely yours and it's your responsibility to find it and hone that skill to the best of your ability.

- Life is not about material things. It's about people, relationships and experiences.

- Try not to be one sided in your thinking. Allow yourself to see all sides of the situation, not just the side that benefits you.

- Don't let people manipulate you and use you. Stand up for yourself and think for yourself.

- Save 10% or more of whatever you make for yourself. Invest it and make sure you get a good return on your investments.

- Meeting someone and falling in love with them is by far one of the most wonderful and exhilarating experiences life has to offer. Sometimes it feels like your breath has been taken away. An involuntary smile that feels like it started from your toes and was pushed through your entire body. The type of nervous energy that makes you feel good and alive. When you're in that moment, embrace it and live in it, because you can't get that time or feeling back.

- Women are the single most outstanding, wonderful, confusing, special, complicated, beautiful, arousing, and fascinating creatures on the planet. Treat them with kindness and respect. But never tolerate a woman that uses you or treats you with disrespect. A good woman will help you and refine your situation, not tear it down or misuse it. A good woman improves your quality of life. She just makes your life better.

- Relationships are not 50/50. They should be 100/100. You have to give your all to a relationship to make it work and your partner should be doing the same. Open communication, honesty, and realistic expectations should be the foundation of any viable relationship.

- Not everyone should have children. If you don't have an overwhelming desire to have kids, do not create a life. It is by far the most difficult job on the planet in my opinion. It's beautifully challenging. Nothing can prepare you for it and there is no secret to success. It is all an experiment, the outcomes are varied.

- If something appears too good to be true, it probably is. Use your instincts and intuition to help guide you through difficult life terrain.

- Write down your goals and aspirations. Set time limits for those goals to keep yourself accountable. Even if you miss deadlines, keep working towards the goal until you accomplish it. Check it off and make another one. Writing your thoughts and goals down serves as a living map. An ever-changing document that will guide you through life. Difficult moments, moments of uncertainty and moments of chaos. It brings clarity and purpose.

- Quiet uneventful moments are moments of peace. Embrace them with an open heart and mind. You will learn a lot about yourself in those moments.

- Life can be loud and chaotic. Sometimes we feel like we need to be constantly entertained by something. Quiet yourself (turn everything off) sometimes to hear what truly needs to be said…or unsaid.

- You know I have a lot of friends (I call them your Uncles) that I love and appreciate very much. They have helped me along my journey in various ways. Keep good people around you. "Iron sharpens

Iron". Having good people with positive things happening in their lives helps elevate you. They bring your property value up. And you should do the same for them. You can learn a lot about a person by the company they keep. Be careful of who you make friends with.

- Try to be an asset and not a liability. Bring valuable skills to the table that will help elevate whatever it is you're trying to accomplish.

- Travel whenever you get the chance. Especially abroad. It changes your perspective, opens your path wider and makes you appreciate life more. I became a different person once I was able to travel abroad. It just tweaks your frequency a bit.

- Drugs and alcohol. You both know I enjoy drinking. I also support marijuana use when applicable. But you have to be careful when indulging in drinking or smoking. If you choose to try it. Not everyone drinks and that is actually more normal than people who do drink. If you decide to engage in it at the appropriate age, make sure you're somewhere safe. Around people you trust. You won't know how your body or mind will react to foreign substances. You have to ensure you're in a safe space. Drinking is not for everyone. Some people just can't and shouldn't indulge in it. Whether it's because they get aggressive, pass out (blackout) or make poor decisions.

- Sex is an activity that you will find extremely pleasurable. It is one of, if not the greatest feeling in life. Connecting with another human being on an intimate level is magnificent. But you have to be careful of the partners you choose. Not everyone deserves your energy and or love. You can't just give it to everyone. You should value your body, mind and your intimacy. Ideally it should be reserved for someone that can match your frequency, someone you can trust and someone you care for and cares for you. But it will also be used recklessly at times. A simple attraction or connection will be all it takes to make you want to engage with them. And you must be careful of those moments. Sexually transmitted diseases and pregnancy is a real possibility every time you engage in unprotected sex. Always use a condom. And be careful of how you share your energy and body. It's special and so are you.

- Learn a skill that will make you invaluable no matter the circumstance.
- You have to work for things to truly be able to appreciate them. If you're not invested and working at it, it won't mean as much to you. It won't hold as

much value. Some things are worth working hard for. That is a universal law.

- All women are wonderful, amazing and intergalactic. But as long as you find someone you love, loves you, communicates with you and respects your value, that's all that matters to me.

- Learn how to properly handle and fire a weapon. There is nothing wrong with knowing how to protect yourself at all levels.

- We've taught you to take care of yourself. Being able to wash clothes, dishes, fold clothes, iron, take out the trash etc. makes you an all-around useful man. We call them chores, but it's just a way of life. Be comfortable with taking care of yourself.

- Don't be mean to people. It's impolite and unnecessary. You never know what people are going through. You also don't know who people are connected to. You could be burning bridges that you didn't even know existed.

- Most things in life require some level of balance. You can't lean too heavy on one side or another. Sometimes you have to be tough, but you don't have to be mean. Honest, but not hurtful.

- Black boys and men have had a long history with police officers. Your immediate objective when encountering an officer is to de-escalate and get out of the situation. It seems silly to have to say out loud, but it's a necessary tool to know. Getting home without incident is of primary concern. Just follow directions.

- Never quit a job before you have a plan for your next move. When you have bills and responsibilities to tend to, it's irresponsible to not have a steady source of income to take care of said responsibilities and debt.

- Intentions tell a lot about a person. Be careful of your intentions with people.

- I'm not perfect. I make a lot of mistakes. And I have never had a problem apologizing for my many missteps. I attempt to be as genuine as I can be. I hope that you have always felt my love and sincerity.

- Honesty is preferred, respect is what you earn and trust is something you gain when loyalty is returned.

- The book, *The Power Of Now* by Eckhart Tolle changed my thought process. Yesterday is gone and tomorrow doesn't exist. The only moment that truly matters is the moment you are living in…in the NOW. It's perfectly ok to plan for tomorrow, but your mind can't live in tomorrow or the past. Stay in the present and embrace that existence.

- Success is not about how much "stuff" you can accumulate. Everyone's idea of success is different. Set your goals realistically and work hard at achieving them. Completing personal or professional goals is a form of success.

- In our current societal state, selfishness feels like it's at an all-time high. You're responsible for your life, but you're expected to assist others along your journey. Humans need each other. Lend a helping hand when you can. Sacrifice personal time to assist another human in need. We're all a part of the human race and the human construct. Volunteer, help the elderly and the youth of this world. They're the most vulnerable. Give of thyself.

- Invest in property, there are options when you own land. Owning land is a superpower. Rent it, lease it, or hold it until it is worth more and sell it.

- Always keep a stash of cash handy for emergencies ($2-3K). Never tell anyone where it is, just have it.

- Know three to four phone numbers by heart in case you lose your phone.

- Paying attention is the most important thing for a driver. No distractions like messing with your phone, playing with your friends, or trying to play music. Driving can be dangerous when you're not paying attention. We always want you and your friends to get home safely. Please pay attention.

- NOBODY…and I mean NOBODY on this planet, will love you more than, or like your mother and me. You can come to us about anything, no matter what it is…no matter how bad you think it is…we will always love you, no matter what. We can work through anything together. Trust us, because we trust in you. We love you.

Forever and for always,

-Dad

RESOURCES BEYOND THE BOOK

Uncharted Territory is a conversation surrounding all things fatherhood and parent related. Many of us are figuring out this parenting thing on the fly. And some of us are questioning if we're doing the right things or not.

I intend to create a support network of men (and women) who want to help each other progress and stand strong as supported dads, parents and partners. *Uncharted Territory* can be used a resource for men's groups, schools, book clubs, sports organizations and for mental health professionals to further the conversation about fatherhood. We need to know that we're not the only ones who feel this way. Some of us need help knowing how to navigate waters that we have never traveled.

I'm available for speaking engagements, podcast interviews, and book club meetings. Feel free to connect with me on social media and leave a review on Amazon, Barnes and Noble or wherever books are sold.

✉ manassehthornton@gmail.com

📞 248-410-4300

📷 Uncharted_territory_manasseh

f Uncharted_territory_manasseh

ACKNOWLEDGEMENTS

Mommy, you are my biggest supporter and fan. You've always told me to write. You would look at me and say, "You need to write, you have something to say." I always listened but I'm a 'lil hard-headed at times, that's why it's taken this long. Thank you for everything. I wouldn't be the man I am without you. You believed in me from the beginning (as many mothers do). You are my biggest influence, role model, and angel.

Dad, Big Bad Bob, AKA Mercy! You gave me the blueprint. You are the foundation that holds up my house. As your son, I couldn't ask for more than that. You taught me how to sacrifice, provide, and find my voice in the wild. Thank you for your sacrifices, hard work, and dedication to our family.

To my big sisters Stacy and Robin. You guys have always been my protectors, and I always looked up to you.

Thank you for always being there for me. I'm so proud of all you have accomplish and the things you continue to do. I love you. To my brothers-in-law Ant and Ed, you have been teaching me lessons since I was a young pup. My sisters are older than me so, my brothers-in-love have been around since I was young. They've showed me discipline, patience, and integrity. I couldn't have asked for better partners for my sisters. I love you brothers.

To my big brother Kamau, baby brother Josh, thanks for being there and always having my back. No matter what's going on, you're always there. Love ya'll.

So many of my friends and family have shaped who I am as a father, it would be sacrilege not to acknowledge some of them in this process. I can't name them all, but they all know who they are because I've told every one of them individually how they've impacted my life. Some of my friends got married and some had children when we were young. Because of their bravery, I was able to witness their successes and failures; it gave me a glimpse into their life and how I want to manage mine.

My friend and brother Chris Amill had his sons when we were younger. He was 21 or 22 when he had his first child, CJ. Shortly after came Tarren. I thought he was crazy as hell for getting married and having kids so early, but his journey isn't my journey. But our friendship allowed me to see firsthand his successes and his failures as a father and husband. The lessons were invaluable. He is a football coach, and his boys were with him all the time. Practices, games, you name it, they were there. His passion, dedication, ups, and downs were on full display for me to learn from. That bond he created with his sons is wonderful to see and is evident to this day. Chris has no idea how much he influenced me and helped me on this path.

I know there is this narrative of Black fathers in society, that we don't stick around and are dead beats, but I push back against that with furious anger. It's a false narrative. Almost every one of my friends and family are amazing fathers and or mentors. They are present, loving, accountable, and productive.

To my brothers, cousins, and friends: Wes, Art, Jason, Damo, Joe, Eric, Ameen, DJ, Mylo, Freeze, Cory, Shaker, Scott, Trev, Dale, Grant, Geno, Manny, Ant, Kev, Joel, Fon, Bryant Parker (rest in peace), Scoop, Christian, and The Brothers of Alpha Phi Alpha Frat. Inc Mighty Xi Chapter…the list goes on. Too many to name. These gentlemen are all amazing fathers and have parented some amazing human beings! They all in some ways influenced me, helped me, supported me, and overall had my back. I learned so much from them! I'm so grateful for them all.

And a special shoutout to my brothers Will L. for creating the cover, Corbin and Kian who put a battery in my back and told me to write this story. This wouldn't have happened without you.

To Penda, thank you for taking my hand and walking me through this experience. There is NO WAY that this is possible without your help. I was lost and you helped me gather my footing. I didn't think I could, and you said, "You will."

And to anyone who has ever helped me, instructed me, cheered me, befriended me…thank you.

www.ingramcontent.com/pod-product-compliance
Lightning Source LLC
Chambersburg PA
CBHW052029030426
42337CB00027B/4928